MAXWELL
PLAYS TWO

Glyn Maxwell

PLAYS TWO

BROKEN JOURNEY
BEST MAN SPEECH
THE LAST VALENTINE

OBERON BOOKS
LONDON

WWW.OBERONBOOKS.COM

First published in 2006 by Oberon Books Ltd

521 Caledonian Road, London N7 9RH

Tel: +44 (0) 20 7607 3637 / Fax: +44 (0) 20 7607 3629

e-mail: info@oberonbooks.com

www.oberonbooks.com

A catalogue record for this book is available from the British Library.

PB ISBN: 9781840026153

E ISBN: 9781786822048

Cover design: Andrzej Klimowski

eBook conversion by Lapiz Digital Services, India.

Visit www.oberonbooks.com to read more about all our books and to buy them. You will also find features, author interviews and news of any author events, and you can sign up for e-newsletters so that you're always first to hear about our new releases.

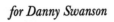

for Danny Swanson

And with special thanks to Jon Croker, Greg Doran,
Paul Garrington, Ben Harrison, Micheline Steinberg, Lloyd Trott,
Suzanne van Lohuizen, Felicity Wren and James Wren.

Contents

Author's Note

- These plays are written in blank verse, so most of the lines are five-beat lines (or pentameters).

- Stage directions are kept to a minimum, and never is any indication given as to how a line should be said, but experience has taught one principle that should be insisted upon: any single line that is shared among two or more characters is still a single line. If spaces are allowed to intervene between the words of separate characters within a line the momentum is fatally harmed. These plays are composed of lines – not sentences or thoughts – and the lines should be kept intact.

- The indications as to ages or genders are guidelines based upon previous stagings; they are not strict instructions.

- All matters of design and costume are entirely in the hands of the producing company. The fact that the language of these plays is, on the face of it, contemporary, should not tempt actors too far into the naturalistic: if they were meant to be read as prose they would be written as prose.

- Words and lines and spaces come where they come for a reason, as in a musical score. There is nothing poetic about these plays aside from that one principle of their construction. They are written in verse not for reasons of aesthetics or culture or nostalgia, but because poets write in verse and a poet wrote these.

BROKEN JOURNEY

adapted from the short story
In a Grove by Ryunosuke Akutagawa

and from the film
Rashomon by Akira Kurosawa

Characters

TROY
a motorcyclist

CHLOE and ANDRE
partygoers

MRS MILLWOOD
a clairvoyante

PAUL
a paper boy

The play occurs in two places and times:
in the small hours of Sunday morning, on a 'Roadside';
and, later that morning, in an interview room at a police 'Station'.

This play was first performed in November 1999 at the Hen and Chickens Theatre Bar, London with the following cast:

TROY, David Peacock
CHLOE, Felicity Wren
ANDRE, Jack Herbert
MRS MILLWOOD, Fiona Welburn
PAUL, Robert Tiffen

Director, Paul Garrington
Designer, Nicky Shaw

Produced by James Wren for Unrestricted View
in association with Toye.

A revised version of this play was first performed on November 12 2005 at Theatre Three, New York with the following cast:

TROY, Craig Smith
CHLOE, Elise Stone
ANDRE, Michael Surabian
MRS MILLWOOD, Sheila O'Malley
PAUL, Joe Rayome

Director, Ted Altschuler
Designer, Narelle Sissons

Produced by Elise Stone for Phoenix Theatre Ensemble.

Scene One

*(A telephone attached to a post. A broken down sports car.
Light on TROY, bloody.)*

TROY: My lawyer says there's no such thing as silence.
    As of now. He says I can't just sit here
    and waste your time any more and I say well,
    more's the pity. Because if I could, you'd be here,
    Officer and your constables of eyeballs,
    until that comet what-is-it arrives,
    blinds us all with science. *Howevah*...my lawyer,
    my lawyer has informed me
    silence nowadays means just the same
    as prattling on forever. You may not know,
    but me I hail from a tribe of silent people,
    and I don't take too kindly being the first
    to 'breach the peace', as you might say, Officer.
    *(Dawn lights up slowly on the car. ANDRE, in his black-tie
    outfit with white silk scarf; CHLOE in her ball-gown and
    shawl. While TROY talks on, ANDRE and CHLOE arrive
    at the Roadside: try the phone, find it's been vandalised, chat,
    argue, drink champagne from paper cups.)*
    If you can read a silence, you can make
    nought plus nought add up to something, I'm thinking,
    and see things where there's no things.
    My lawyer recommends in this case I
    don't keep silent, silence now not meaning
    No I've no thoughts at all on your dead man
    skewered in his Sunday best, but meaning
    something like...I'm Troy:
    somebody came to grief, you look for me,
    your favourite suspect hereabouts. If need be
    you ride me off my sodding bike so I get
    cuts and laceration, look at it, blood hey
    that's got a guilty colour, just the same
    as what you scraped this morning off your chap

in his tuxedo, tails and that. In the silence
a picture's getting drawn and it stars Troy.
I stopped, and 'cause I'm Troy I stabbed that man,
say 'cause he's rich, let's say, or 'cause I fancy
his car. Talking of *fancy*, by and by
you'll find, you don't know this, this shimmering lady
all flustered running about like Cinderella,
her driver turned to pumpkin in the small hours.
By all means fall in love but don't believe her.
You will, though, I can see it, it won't be me.
My picture's almost done, hung up for sale.
Seeing I'm Troy and seeing I keep my silence
I murdered him for a buzz, I screwed his girlfriend,
and, what a nice touch, even swiped their *bubbleh*!
Wasn't I swigging it when your poncey Panda
ran me off the road? So you can have me
on murder, rape and, whoops, drink-driving. I tell you,
the way the judges are these days it's that,
drink-driving that'd send you down, not raping,
not once you tell m'lud about the ball-gown.
So there's your picture, Officers assembled.
Sign it, like you do, and hang it where
you wish I hanged, but *I am here to tell you*
something's missing. Something's always missing.
Every time you open up your toy-box
for clues and prints and alibis and shite
it's always missing. My lawyer's shaking his head,
but that's because it's missing in his world,
it's nicked from all your worlds. And the thing's Love.
Love's that missing part. It's what you miss
whenever there's a silence. But it means
you'll never understand a single thing
that happens round my life if you can't see it.
– What do you mean, 'Is that why I had to kill him?'
Love's why he had to go, it's not the same
but you've got what you want. You don't want *why*.
You don't want *why*, and *why's* where you find Love.

Fair do-s, Officer Scribble, I'm confessing
to Love in the first degree. And if your friend
is well-dressed in a ditch and he'll never pass
the sherry again to the vicar on his left
or brandy is it, I'm sorry, and his fair lady
is floating over the Downs in a right old sulk,
yes I'm the cause of it all, but the cause of that
is Love. I'll show you the difference
between your filthy picture you're so proud of,
and a tale of Love I'm prouder of by miles.
You look at me like you never saw a girl
pass by you and you wanted to have her always.
You never did? Then this might as well be silence.
(*TROY moves into the background, beside the story.*)

ANDRE: It's not what you said before.

CHLOE: I changed my view,
frankly.

ANDRE: How nice was it seven miles from London?
You can't see lights or houses?

CHLOE: There's a place,
I went there. Well. I've gone right off the idea.
They really ought to fill the space with something.
A little hut with a fire, Andre. Blankets.
An ice-bucket, why not? That's my civilised
initiative for outposts.

ANDRE: What I'd build
on this particular outpost is a signpost
saying 'ESSO'.

CHLOE: 'M1'.

ANDRE: M anything.
What do you think are the odds against a whole
acre of country being by accident
overlooked, I mean always, since Domesday
through Magna Carta, railways, elections,
I mean always, so by accident there's a place
existing in the Dark Ages?

CHLOE: The odds?
Nine zillion to one. But the odds against
you running out of bloody petrol in it –
evens, sunshine.

ANDRE: It's possible in theory.
That soldier in Japan.

CHLOE: Yes, that's right, sweetheart,
console yourself that somewhere on this planet
someone is feeling a bigger jerk than you are.

ANDRE: You're sounding unhelpful, Chloe.

CHLOE: On second thoughts
he can survive in jungles, and he thinks
he's still at war, while you won't last a day
without a toothbrush and a trouser-press.
Not to mention a shag.

TROY: (I heard all this.
I'll tell you how, but first I'll tell you why.)

CHLOE: Let's have a drink.

TROY: Always one for a drink...
I was riding and the road was clear as like,
ocean, you know? Like nothing at all, that hour.
I saw them way ahead where the road's straight,
I got to them where it curves and you see the chalk
on either side, that stretch? I come up along,
and I look across, and I'm interested, why not?
Fast car, brand new, now where could they be off to?
I'm thinking, thought I'd take them on the inside,
show them, so, if you picture it, I'm like
I'm glancing and the passenger window slowly
winds itself to its open state and I'm like
I'm staring in this passenger's blue eyes,
whatever colour, she's staring as much as I am
at ninety miles an hour, you know? And she's not
the slightest bit taking notice of who's driving,
and I didn't care myself, though I didn't hate him,
not then, or really ever, it was his girlfriend,

Chloe, I know now, sticks her, her tongue right out
and winds the window up. Me I'm so – shocked
actually, I slow down and drop back,
grin, what with her making the face, *Chloe*,
and follow them like way back, so they know I'm there,
but I change my view, you know, I'm not going to scare her,
freak her out like I could, or going to hurt her.
Then suddenly I lose them, they're gone,
they must have took the exit while I'm grinning,
I have to turn, like a U-ey, you know, ride back,
thinking it's hopeless but it bleeding wasn't hopeless,
Officer, seeing as how they only made it
half a mile beyond the slip road. Ha!
I see the car way off and kill my engine.
It's quiet, it's dreamlike even, and I'm thinking I'll
go up to them for a joke, make a joke of her
laughing at me, I'll have a laugh with those two,
it's not a crime to do that, so I like I
chain the bike up, tiptoe down, you see me,
and there they are, and the one I know she's in this
gown, like silk ball gown like you never see
outside of a flaming wedding meal, or a banquet!
Shining away, it is, and it's still night-time.
Then I'm thinking what shall I say and it comes to me
to be limping, say I'm hurt, it comes to me
to lie to them about my real condition.
CHLOE: Andre, someone. Oh pig. It's only that biker.
ANDRE: Oh marvellous, the Middle of Nowhere Chapter
    of Hell's Angels.
TROY: (You see that to them at first
    I'm just some no one? I tag along with that.)
CHLOE: What's the matter? Fall off your little bike?
ANDRE: You're drunk. Be doubly careful what you say.
CHLOE: Right on, sarge, that's just what I'll doubly do.
TROY: (Up close I couldn't look at her. I had to
    'address my remarks', as you might say, to him.)
    Look at my ankle bone! (is how I started).

ANDRE: Broken, is it?

TROY: Well it doesn't fucking function.
    Mind my language, miss.

CHLOE: Oh it missed me,
    your language.

ANDRE: Can it, Chloe. Don't mind her,
    she's sloshed, aren't you? We went to this event.

TROY: I passed you, didn't you see me? I said: 'Them,
    they went to that event.'

CHLOE: You didn't pass us.
    You hung along like some old hungry seagull
    sniffing for fish.

TROY: You got me wrong, *Madame*,
    sniffing for fizz, more like. I saw you at it,
    knocking it back like a good 'un.

CHLOE: Give him a drink,
    Andre.

TROY: Andre? You French?

CHLOE: My arse he is.

ANDRE: Our wheels ran out of juice.
    And no, we haven't a spare, nor any idea
    where the hell we are, *or* where there's a phone.

TROY: Beside you, squire.

ANDRE: One that bloody works.
    This is the bastard bloody Turner Prize.
    (*ANDRE assaults the public phone.*)

TROY: That's probably how it happened.

CHLOE: Now we know.

TROY: So where's your what-is-it handheld model then?
    You look that kind of guy.

ANDRE: I am that kind.
    We date the girls who leave the blasted things
    behind in cloakrooms.

CHLOE: Hands up who's that kind!

TROY: Well my name's Troy.

ANDRE: Really.

TROY: And you've no phone.

ANDRE: No phone, no map, no food, as it happens.

CHLOE: Not even
    waitress service, can you imagine? And all
    because I left his phone in a safe place.
    That was the cause of the petrol spillage, and,
    of Andre leaving all his maps behind.
    Even your ankle, Mr Troy, that was me,
    naughty bad bad Chloe.

TROY: You're dead right,
    mate, she's really tanked. But any road,
    I'm from round here, I know where there's a phone.

ANDRE: You do? That's brilliant.

CHLOE: Jolly clever of you.

TROY: I'm ninety-nine per cent, it's over this hill,
    along a stretch, and just where the road curves
    across it's like this marshy field, it's there,
    right or left, you'll see it. You know, old style,
    red with a door, like in the good old days,
    operator, operator, like, listed.

ANDRE: How long a trek?

TROY: It won't get any darker.
    Ten minutes' worth of trek.

CHLOE: You run it, Andy.

(*ANDRE draws CHLOE aside.*)

TROY: (So then they like start talking, as if it's a secret!
    He won't go, 'cause it leaves her here with me,
    and *I* can't go in my condition – see,
    that's why I'm limping – all falls into place!
    So she's the one, and they're whispering, and it's like
    speak up, it's Troy's Plan anyway, no secrets!
    See how it happens?)

CHLOE: I've been selected for duty,
    Mr Troy. If this was a film we were in,
    you'd never see me again except in flashback,
    waving, fading away, and you'd say grimly
    'That was the last I saw of her, officer...'

ANDRE: Chloe,
    do can it, you know exactly why you're going.

CHLOE: Oh no, mine's not to reason. Mine's to go
across the pissing peasant-inhabited
Midlands (no offence, mate) at that hour
the psychos go out jogging, and I'm armed
with a giggle, and a lighter. If you find
some village idiot hanged with red suspenders
I'll be Most Wanted, Dead or Alive.
ANDRE: There's no one,
for crying out loud. And look there's this chap's ankle.
CHLOE: Kiss it better, you know you want to. *Ciao.*
    (*CHLOE goes on her mission. An uneasy silence.*)
TROY: You two married? You two look fit to be married.
I'm happy the way I am. I never met
anyone's going to change that way of feeling...
(I'm prattling on like this, as if I'm some
loser on the road – if he only knew
what I'm thinking or how fast I'm thinking!
Out of the way, she is, now on to the next...
No need to hurt this *chap*, just ease him gently
out of commission a while. He'll understand.
Once in his life he must have had to have had her.
And me, I'm feeling so much Love there's Love
like leaking out to him, and I want to kill him
'cause him, he's with her day and night, but I'm saying
I'm liking him!) Andre.
What's with this Andre shit, if you're not French?
ANDRE: I dropped the W, obviously.
TROY: Yeah right.
    Obviously.
ANDRE: There you go.
TROY: Andre...
My first name is Des. Des. Des Troy.
I dropped the Des. (That's actually some old
line I do in pubs, but he's not to know.)
ANDRE: We'll give you a ride to the hospital, okay?
You did give us directions.

TROY: Makes no odds.
   You gave me a slug of fizz.
ANDRE: It's flat by now.
   (*TROY limps to the phone.*)
TROY: Of course if this only worked like a good phone
   and not like you say some bastard prize they give,
   I'd be reading the pissing *Sport* by now with a couple
   of nice young nurses. You and Chloe, well,
   you'd be home in bed together (and you know,
   it's hurting me to say this stuff, but he's got to
   think I'm happy with that.)
ANDRE: Well yes we would be.
TROY: Andre. Why'd you drop the W?
   Was it bothering you?
ANDRE: You oughtn't to stand up,
   weight on the ankle.
TROY: *Eight* on the ankle, that is,
   Andre, thought I'd drop that *W.*
ANDRE: Look,
   piss off.
TROY: Come again, Andy?
ANDRE: You heard, piss off. As in: that's an old joke,
   it's getting a tad tiresome, hence piss off.
   Said with a yawn. Not necessarily hostile.
TROY: Is that right? So it's like what, a pleasantry?
ANDRE: A middle of the bloody night to a helpful stranger
   pleasantry, let's call it.
TROY: I think I get you.
   I think I'm with you at your event, Andre.
   What was it then, your event?
ANDRE: A reunion ball.
   Snakecharmers, it's a society I belong to,
   for my sins.
TROY: So, Chloe, is she a member?
ANDRE: No, a guest. Why? Do you want to join?
TROY: Just wondered. So. You bought her a ticket then?
ANDRE: Christ, it had silver lace. How far's this phone?

TROY: Sensational girl in a gown, old red phone-box,
    they'll find each other no stress.
ANDRE: Right, if she's lost
    the box will come and fetch her.
TROY: You don't know
    this county, do you, Andre?
ANDRE: Blissfully no.
TROY: Anyway, squire, you don't need your lady
    in a big red box or not. I can fix the wiring.
ANDRE: What?
TROY: It's loose. You mean you never looked?
ANDRE: Of course I damn well didn't. I wanted to make
    an emergency telephone call, not show my lover
    I know my earth from neutral.
TROY: Do you, though?
ANDRE: No, but that's not the point. It should be working.
    I pay for it, after all.
TROY: That's jolly decent.
ANDRE: Oh, do the voice.
TROY: I get the brown one wrong.
    Shouldn't matter. Come and hold this a sec.
    I got a Philips somewhere.
ANDRE: Really? Good grief,
    There are such people.
TROY: There's only one of us left.
    (*ANDRE holds a wire down. TROY produces a pair of handcuffs*
    with which he chains ANDRE to the pole, then walks away.)
ANDRE: Okay. Okay. Let's not let any more happen,
    Troy. All right? Okay? Pleasantry? Listen...
    My pocket to the front on the right has about
    forty quid in it, Gold Card, shit, the lot.
    Right? Now the car. When Chloe comes back we will both
    walk very quickly away and forget we ever
    drove in it, you are with me? There. Your car.
    When you make it go it can go with you. Okay?
TROY: (Big deal. But of course there's more, he kept recalling
    all things he had in his world could make me like this

Rocker-bleeding-feller of hereabouts,
his clubs and passes to things. Some toss he must've
given about his life he seemed so keen
to load that crap on me. Now what you're thinking
is, 'What's his business carting round some handcuffs?
That's our function, isn't it?' Well you watch me
do your work for you!) Andre, I'm sorry.
I'm going to have to citizen's-arrest you.
ANDRE: You're what?
TROY: I'd do the speech but I don't know it.
You certainly have the right to remain…there.
Anything else may be, I don't know, taken away
or something. It's for driving under the booze.
ANDRE: You're a pissing policeman now?
TROY: No. Concentrate.
It's citizen's arrest. I'm one of you,
but I always had this moral streak in the veins
and I can't let you load up and just drive off,
mowing down the villagers.
ANDRE: You're right.
Okay. I don't believe this thing is happening
but, technically, you're right. I'm over the line.
Good job, Troy, good job. Now take my keys
and put them in your pocket. I won't drive.
You've done your duty. Then, if it's no trouble,
unlock this damned chain. You make me feel
like a blasted criminal.
TROY: That's the point you see.
You see the chaps in suits all in the nick
who never hurt a fly for this very crime.
It's thoughtlessness and no, I can't unlock you.
We're going by the book.
ANDRE: What cunting book?
TROY: The book of how it's done. I don't know you.
I don't know you're not armed.
ANDRE: I don't know *you're* not.

TROY: Well then I'll tell you. I am, with an army dagger,
    since you enquire.

ANDRE: Oh, so I have that right?
    Look Troy, I trust you, you're right to detain me, yes,
    but what I'm saying is look. The offer stands,
    there's money, plastic, the car. To just forget it,
    turn a blind eye, Christ, policemen do it!

TROY: Do they now? (You don't, do you?)

ANDRE: Troy,
    I don't like this and I don't think it's legal.
    (*TROY approaches him, but forgets to limp.*)

TROY: Don't jolly lecture me on legal, Andre.
    What are you staring at?
    All right, so it's not broken. It's just bruised.
    I'm biting back the pain, Andre. You think
    I'd fake a limp to do my duty, do you?
    We're not all of us snakecharmers, sunshine.

ANDRE: Chloe.

TROY: Right, who could've been your victim,
    face up in a ditch with the wheels spinning.
    (*Enter CHLOE.*)

CHLOE: Well that was a topping amble. What are you doing?

ANDRE: I've been arrested, darling, it's okay,
    he's undercover, he got us, drink and driving.
    Bad start to Sunday, yes. We have to wait.
    D'you call the RAC?

CHLOE: There's not a phone.
    This guy's bullshitting us.

ANDRE: Steady, Chloe, he's…
    (*CHLOE notices the handcuffs.*)

CHLOE: What the hell are you doing?
    You can't do that, unlock him!

TROY: I'm sorry, sweetheart,
    the Law's the Law.

CHLOE: Fuck you, unlock him!

TROY: Careful!

(*CHLOE attacks TROY and they fight. He overpowers her and
they lie there exhausted, he pinning her down.*)

CHLOE: Somebody kissed your ankle better, no?

Or you're this effing fibber, Mr Troy.

TROY: Andy, do you think that?

ANDRE: No I don't think that.

TROY: Your lover doesn't agree.

CHLOE: He's not my lover.

TROY: He says he is. You not her lover, Andy?

Then sorry, who's that make an effing fibber?

Why d'you stick your tongue out at me, Chloe?

CHLOE: Looked out the window, saw this six year-old

pedalling his big bike. Couldn't be helped.

TROY: What do you think of that, Andre?

ANDRE: Don't know.

CHLOE: Go on, you're going to teach me manners, right?

Forget it, look it's daylight,

time to take your ball home, Mr Troy.

(*TROY kisses her.*)

ANDRE: Troy, this is not fair, this is not on.

This isn't happening. Christ!

Chloe, are you all right?

CHLOE: Well I'm not dead.

I think I have a fan club.

TROY: Andy, old son,

it's best you close your eyes and have a snooze.

No one's going to be hurt, but it can't be helped.

Some things just come along they have to be,

they have to be, eh Chloe?

CHLOE: I wouldn't say so.

TROY: She's seen my knife, old son.

CHLOE: He has a knife.

TROY: That's right, you keep him posted. Tell him now

we're going into the car.

CHLOE: I think we'd better.

ANDRE: You better, darling, I'm sorry.

TROY: He's saying he's sorry,

Chloe.

27

CHLOE: Forget it, darling.

TROY: It comes along,
   you can't say no somehow.

CHLOE: No somehow.

TROY: You see? You asleep, Andre? Now he's asleep.
   We'll go on a Sunday drive.
   (*TROY and CHLOE get into the car, which rocks. Light on
   PAUL.*)

PAUL: The first person
   to say about is Mr Troy, the bike fan.
   He came as a surprise, when they were quiet,
   but what he did was ask too many questions
   which tangled them all up, I think, including
   even him. He was riding about so early
   because he couldn't sleep – which was unlike me.
   They were definitely not happy on their own though,
   the two of them, he came at them from nowhere
   it might as well have been. He was a dancer,
   a smoker, and a music fan. He also
   liked football, Aston Villa, and he told them
   before the fight, he told them he was a hundred!
   The two of them they did though
   pay attention to him, which maybe was all
   he wanted them to do, and they also answered
   all the things he asked. It's like they had to
   answer, as if they'd rather
   be with him and answer him than lose him,
   however much it hurt them both to have to.
   (*TROY emerges from the car.*)

TROY: (How d'you like my story, Officer sir?
   I bet you like it fine, it's time at last
   to nail me up for false imprisonment, rape,
   whatever. But you're wrong and you're always wrong,
   picking at my images, some jackdaw
   you only want the worms you know. You don't want
   that she began to kiss me, you don't want
   she tugged her wedding-cake dress up, do you, in there,

or pulled me at her quicker than you'd credit,
or that she bustled round like a bird in a great
cloud of this white nest, and you don't want
she wanted me and clawed at me and see this?
You test it, that's my blood, that is, not hers,
not his, not hers, and done in the heat of something
you don't want to believe. That she could love me,
once, for a second in some dark stinking place
she loved me. Technically, as Andre would say.
And what I say to you I said to him...)
I know what you're thinking, chum. The answer's no.
I didn't. Some things you love too much to love
the way they want you to. Your woman –

ANDRE: She's not
that.

TROY: – I love that way.
I'm leaving her to you. It's what she wants.
She may not know it now but it's for the best.
(And sir, it hurt to do that, knowing now
she loved me like I loved her. But I had to.
It's like I said, some things just come along
you can't say no. But that's not in your world,
officer, is it? You know I loved those two
just then...)
(*CHLOE gets out of the car.*)

ANDRE: Are you okay,
Chloe, are you okay?

TROY: Answer your man.

CHLOE: Crawl away and die.

TROY: You answer him.

CHLOE: Look I'm okay, Andre. There's no harm done.
You going to leave us now, Troy, just ride off?
Some sort of hobby, is it?

TROY: That's my style,
Chloe.

CHLOE: What about him? You're going to free him?
He'll kill you, Troy. You'll kill him, won't you, Andre?

29

He does that officer training stuff, don't you,
Andre, and all that eastern shit. He'll kill you.

ANDRE: Try and stop me.

CHLOE: See?

TROY: Then let him try. Fair fight. Man against man.

CHLOE: And what's the prize?

TROY: You are.
He wins, I'm gone for good.
I win, you ride with me wherever I'm headed.

CHLOE: I say. Dear, what do you say?

ANDRE: I say unlock me.
I'm ready.

TROY: (See, Officer sir,
my friend, no one believes any more in honour,
do they? Look, I was cacking it. This geezer
for all I know is this black belt in whatever
they give black belts for. Me, I'm just this scrapper.
Look after myself and that. But it was for Chloe.
A last good deed, if you like. I had this sense
the guy was gone up here, he was going to kill her.)
Unlock him, Chloe. Then you better stand clear.

(*TROY gives her the key to the handcuffs. She unlocks ANDRE.*)

CHLOE: Darling, I –

ANDRE: Don't touch me.
Throw your knife down, Troy.

TROY: The knife is down.

CHLOE: Darling, careful –

ANDRE: Stay out of my sight-line.

TROY: (I could see now I had to win. If I went down
her life wasn't worth living. Officer sir,
believe this if it's all you can believe:
at that moment I prayed. Then he was on me.)

(*TROY and ANDRE fight, cleanly at first. Then ANDRE picks up the knife. TROY wrests it back and stabs ANDRE, who staggers to the pole and slides down it. TROY finds that CHLOE has run away.*)

Ask me again. I'll say again don't ask me.

She ran away. Perhaps she couldn't face
the thing she'd done, who knows. I learned about her
too late for it to help me. Yes I killed him,
if as you say he's dead. But I never meant to.
I struck in self-defence. It was my idea
to fight with these, it's him who breaks the glass   (*Fists.*)
and swings the silverware. And I never hurt her.
Would you? I mean, do you know what she looks like?
(*Enter CHLOE to the Station, distressed.*)
You do? You got her here? Well then you know then.
She's an awful beauty, Constable, you let her
look at you she'll have you. Let her go now,
I strongly recommend, or else she'll do it,
she'll make the face at you, she'll make you need her,
need to follow her, crave her,
you won't do what you want again, you'll love her
and say so, even you, you'll make a statement,
you'll note: 'Hi was pro-ceeding through me life,
when suddenly' – next moment you'll be scrapping,
crying, and I can't help you
any more than this I'm saying. Remember:
what means the world to you and me is something
she doesn't even know she's done. You lose her.
Give her a cup of tea and good directions,
south until she drowns in all that *bubbleh.*
She passed by me. I wanted to have her always.
So now I'm screwed for always. So that's fair.
Tell her that when you see her. That's my statement.

Scene Two

(*CHLOE at the Station.*)

CHLOE: It started when in school the day they gave me
options about I was doing English already
they said I could do now French or I could do German
politely they said but I did a different option
what with English and science and maths and games
I did a different language option. Laura
Laura took French and Joy took German and I took
I took having those options my own language
called 'Yes Language' and it's very very it's easy
it's easy to learn it you all you have to learn
is how you can make out of any word or letters
in English the word *yes*. Whatever you say,
what happens to you ever in life you have only
to open your mouth and it trots out *yes, yes* –
This can be done at any function. Such as
boardrooms, or the buffets you hear it. Then later
at a higher level you learn it's not even words it's
also *nothing* means *yes* and if you're a master
which I am, you learn you can be just your body
dead or alive, and it's still
yes you're saying whatever you're saying. Pardon?
Yes I can talk, I'm calm, I'm only explaining
my language so you can understand my culture
and why this is blood and I'm filthy it's just my culture.
Who did you find? That's clever, you found that one.
What happened? You know what happened look at my face.
Where? In a blue blue place and it's un-, it's un-,
unfrequented. Today this was, a man drinking
wine from somewhere? The man appears the man
on a motor a motorcycle. He starts becoming
friendly when Andre?…Andre saw him that's right
he says, 'Here's a Knight of the Road…'

That's the phrase, the choice phrase he employs
later, the man I mean, 'I'm a Knight of the Road...'
Petrol's what it was. Why we were there
and he must have said he knew a place for petrol?
Petrol. This happened because we ran out of petrol
ha! Whose fault is that superintendent, super
petrol intendent? Iraqis? Iraqis...
Iraqis with car-keys? Ha ha ha...
I'm sorry, huh, I'm sorry with my Iraqis...
I went to go for the – what do you say here
what can you say in English, the double-you-see?
The *ladies*, the officers' mess?! I like the *ladies*,
the *ladies*. Yes, I needed to go to the *ladies*.
Yes I want to go there now, I need a *yes*.
I'm going to yes to the *ladies* for a yes
and yes you can yes with me if you want to yes,
you superintendents, we'll all yes to the *ladies*...
(*Exit CHLOE. ANDRE rises up the pole, still chained to it.*
Enter CHLOE to the Roadside.)
Andre, what are you doing?
(*TROY jumps out.*)

TROY: I'm the surprise.
CHLOE: What the fuck – what is this –
ANDRE: Chloe be quiet,
    he might go away.
TROY: I might never go away.
ANDRE: I'm chained to the pole, Chloe, I can't do a thing.
CHLOE: You're chained to the pole?
TROY: He's chained to the pole, Chloe.
    He can't do a thing.
CHLOE: So bloody unchain him. Now.
TROY: No.
ANDRE: It's okay, Chloe.
CHLOE: It's not okay.
TROY: It is okay. That's 2-1 for Okay.
    After extra time.

CHLOE: What do you want?
  No...
TROY: 'It's okay, Chloe.' Isn't it, Andy?
  Isn't it, Andy?
ANDRE: It is. Don't worry about me.
CHLOE: Don't worry about *you*?
TROY: He said. Don't worry about him.
  He's like that, Andy.
CHLOE: *No!*
TROY: He said don't worry.
CHLOE: *No, no, no!*
  (*TROY draws his knife and goes after CHLOE. This fight is*
  ugly, dirty, short. TROY drops the knife and forces CHLOE into
  the car. Light on PAUL.)
PAUL: The second person to say about is called
  Chloe, and I think that she was an odd
  kind of lady, usually saying a thing
  you didn't quite expect but understand though,
  but after she'd said it. She made both the men
  pleased and furious too and often both things.
  Her smile was different though, she only really
  smiled when they weren't looking at her, something
  I have never see before, that is, and of course
  she didn't know that sometimes she was smiling
  right in my direction. If she had known that
  she would have stopped, to stop her smile being seen.
  She would have smiled at me like at the men.
  That would have scared me, or maybe made me sad.
  She looked like she had just been at her own
  marriage and Andre was not the husband.
  (*CHLOE re-emerges, at the Station again.*)
CHLOE: Thank you, ladies, thank you. I had a need
  and now I don't. It was a need inside me
  it tugged me like a little thing and I told it,
  'You can be free, little thing,' and now it's free
  until the next little thing that I hear a voice
  squeaking in there, 'Let me be free as well...'

And that will be free and again there'll just be me,
Chloe, Chloe the cage, Chloe the casket.
But I know men so fat with the little things
they creak and they can't walk and they need cars
or darkness or doctors
to set them free and they free them into Chloe
who says in her *yes language* yes they are welcome
cordially to the ladies' animal zoo
to feed on ladies always the little things,
endangered frightening biting little things so
so come and see them, all of you come and see them
don't worry about the moat how it's all red
and salty a man can cross it, he can wade
smiling here in his wellingtons to watch
and point out things to children.
(*She sees ANDRE watching the car, unconscious of her. She goes to
him.*)   What are you watching?
Is this a model you wish to purchase from us?
Look how it goes. Look at your open eyes,
young gentleman, you can drive it away this morning…
(*CHLOE goes to the car, takes out her ball-gown, which she puts on.*)
Here comes the owner now. Uh-oh, she's a woman.
So good or bad, young gentleman, a woman?
Does it mean not many miles on the clock, a woman?
Or maintenance a problem, or the bodywork
neglected, rusted even? Will she be honest?
She needs to sell this, look at her, this woman
driver, owner, seller. Look at her eyes.
She doesn't seem to know where she is now, does she?
A car-yard, that's man's territory, she knows it,
don't you reckon? You'll ride away the richer.
I think she intends to do a deal. Now remember,
confidence. Remember the end in sight
and wipe away what's *in* the way. Now. Deal…
(*CHLOE takes off the gown. TROY gets out of the car, throws
ANDRE the key to the handcuffs, then leaves. CHLOE picks
up the key and starts to unlock ANDRE.*)

I'm going to, have to, unlock you because you have to
go somewhere to get
go somewhere to get some people some others
with help, if I unlock you you have to do that
it's only fair…
ANDRE: It's only fair, she says.
A very fair bargain, I'd say.
CHLOE: What do you say…
ANDRE: A very fair bargain, I said. And that, to be honest,
is my last word on the matter.
CHLOE: What does it mean…
(*CHLOE goes back to the room at the Station.*)
His name is Andrew Linley, or, Andre.
Friend of a friend, I don't know where those come from.
There's I think a land of them, they know each other,
they compliment each other's taste in us.
Friend of a friend. There's a whole America of them.
I met him at lunch, he was a buyer he
he asked me out I went. To a Mexican.
He showed me round the Mexican green menu.
And how to hold my glass and for five weeks
I've been with him. The people I knew before
they moved them somewhere else there was a mix-up I
I found myself on a bed with the world spinning
and him at the end of it thrilled and saying 'and now'
and always what he said was next *was* next.
He's rich you understand… What does *what* mean?
Snakecharmers? That's a society of men,
in rooms that are candle-lit, their faces flicker.
Snakecharmers. They let the *ladies* in
and passed us round like a light – 'I've got one somewhere!'
Snakecharmers. One word. You found some tickets?
Oh yes it was yesterday. The day of yes-es.
Last night? No, we had not had *those* relations.
I'm not like him I don't have the money to always
be dined and dance and wear such a dress I wore there!
Cinderella…you know, finally, goes there.

I felt so – I felt so –
he's there at my back he's always there and he's saying
I know a place and they *always always* know one
I know a place and he's drunk and dragging me off to the
you've probably got one officers, *patio*
to the patio and he wants us sssssskedaddling off
on to the lawn you know but I'm in my gown,
my gown, I want to *dance*, frankly, frankly
that's all. He doesn't believe me so he boozes
until it's the Middle Ages and it's his right!
So he tries again and I try again in my language
but it sounds the same in ancient English and so
so we have to leave in the car, we have to go south
(*CHLOE goes back to the Roadside.*)
south to your country, superintending ladies,
where you are asking, 'Who
has hurt a man this morning? Is it her?'
You know how my language sounds, you know the answer.
Listen then, like ladies,
it's only fair.

ANDRE: It's only fair, she says.
A very fair bargain, I'd say.

CHLOE: What do you say…

ANDRE: A very fair bargain, I said. And that, to be honest,
is my last word on the matter.

CHLOE: What does it mean…
(*ANDRE gets free of the handcuffs and approaches CHLOE.*)
What do you mean, Andre, it's your last word?
What are you doing, why are you staring at me?
Say something, Andre, you have to!
(*They fight. CHLOE finds Troy's knife. When ANDRE catches
her and bears down upon her, she stabs him. He staggers back
to the pole and slides down it. CHLOE returns to the room in
the Station.*)
A single word would have done it.
So many he had to choose from and me I had
my *yes* or nothing. His language failed him. I swear

he only had to have said… But that one wanted
something so very hurt to be speaking for him,
a thing so sick and old he was full of. Boys.
They're always loping after you in the dark.
They're always crying out, you can always hear them.
Even their silence eats you away, it's salt.
What blood and water. All *my* blood and water?
Ha-ha, it's all I'm made of. That and this spit I
I get in my eyes and tears like stuck in my throat?
This? Hm, this is blood from a slit I made
on a long road sign on both this wrist and that wrist.
On a road sign… And, and, the water
well that's from when I drowned in a moat you dug
nearby to here to stop me arriving. I made
efforts to take no more of your precious time,
instead you frankly get a ruined Sunday
slogging down my river. Because I'm afraid I'm
I'm afraid you can't kill Cinderella. And now
I'm finished with my language look it got me
nowhere, it got me here with you, and if that's
what it was for, then it's finished, fine. You can call it
the Lost Tongue of Chloe, and you can call me
sarcophagus and queue for hours to see me,
but you can't touch or you can but I won't know you.

Scene Three

(*Lights up on ANDRE, 'dead'. From off, TROY and CHLOE, laughing. MRS MILLWOOD comes, with things of Andre's: the scarf, the invite, his keys. She makes herself comfortable, helps herself to tea. The laughter fades. When she speaks Andre's words, she does so in his voice.*)

MILLWOOD: It's kind of you, I know – these are they,
    digestives as required and I'm grateful,
    as per the yellow form, but I'm not simple.
    I'm perfectly aware that as I sit here
    I'm sailing into general amusement
    at what I am. Now you may hear a silence,
    and think yourself the soul of *politesse*,
    sergeant, but you're screaming, don't deny it,
    and don't think for a moment that I mind that.
    I mean, it's not a question of belief,
    of yours or mine or theirs, it's more a question
    of what you want to hear. I'll tell you things
    that are being said around us as we speak,
    and if you wish to listen you may do so,
    and if you wish to laugh no one can stop you.
    I see the bind you're in. Inspector Browning
    wants me here, and would like me tape-recorded
    while he's out hunting clues. Now this upsets you,
    it isn't in the manual, but he wants it.
    Instead of the evidence? No. As well as the evidence.
    Well, why not. Now all he'll find out there
    is what's been left behind to make new patterns.
    Whereas, this is happening now,
    around, among you...Andrew Morrison Linley.
    Keys to many different places. A scarf,
    he likes the scarf. An invitation card.
    He didn't stay here long, did he, at this place...
    'We'll have to make a pit stop.' Did you hear that?
    He had to leave the road, and he had a sense

something was botched. He's made a kind of friend
somehow and it's bothering him. He's bothered,
Andrew, he's terribly – bothered. He died slowly,
didn't he, yes he did and he didn't mean to.
He's stressing that, he didn't mean to. He's angry,
I'm sorry, it's going to be tough, a little, he really
isn't happy. We'll wind it back a little,
just like your tape-recorder, really, a rewind.
Before he's made his friend. 'What do you think' –
(*ANDRE starts to slide up the pole, then leaves it and stands free.*)
'What do you think are the odds against' – then something
something about 'this country', something 'accident'
he's asking a question, uses the word – 'Domesday
through Magna Carta,' something something, 'elections…
always, so by accident there's a place
existing in the Dark Ages,' he's asking,
he's out of doors, it's cold where he asks – *her* that,
I'm sorry, this can't be helping, I do think
he loves a girl and can't think how to please her.
(*CHLOE comes to the car; ANDRE returns to the pole.*)
I'll budge along, there's only two of them, no,
there's someone else and when he's there it's warmer
somehow, what that *could* mean is there's music,
yes or maybe animals? I think music.
(*TROY comes to the car. ANDRE reaches and pockets the fallen
knife.*)
Dancing. Dancing. Yes, and a great love,
I mean it, a gust, a gale, I mean! From him,
but he can't say it quite or he can't move?
I don't think he can move – it's either that
or he can't speak his heart. He says nothing –
no, what he's saying is: 'Nothing took a while
and a half that time. Nothing took a while
and a half that time.' And he is so very bothered.
And this is where it starts, that is, the end,
starts just about right now. Wait. A ballpoint.
No a knife. He has a knife and he believes

it's going to help him leave the place he's in.
It does, but not exactly as he planned it.
'Ha-bloody-ha. Score one for cool Andre,
forty thou a year, a Toyota, pad
in Notting Hill, a Snakecharmer and hello!
I've come back as your gran. That just about
clinches a fine outing. How was your night,
Andre? Oh, the usual. Took my girlfriend
to a ninety-five pound ball but didn't snog her.
Ran out of gas in the Land that Time Forgot.
Got matey with Cro-Magnon Man, who thought he'd
chain me to a broken phone-box, let him
haul said girlfriend into car and shag her,
watch them have a fag and a fight and scarper,
then died and got a call from an old Doris
chomping away on a Rich Tea. How was yours?
Bothered. Wouldn't you be a *soupçon* bothered?
Christ knows what they're saying happened. At least
someone wants to knows the truth. Oh yeah laugh,
fine, but why would I lie? What's my motive?
I'll tell you what sodding happened. Are you listening?
Are you there? See now, I have to sodding say it,
don't I? Are you there? Ha-bloody-ha.'
(*CHLOE gets out of the car, smoking a cigarette.*)

CHLOE: Don't look at me like that. You're in a mood.
I hate it when you do that.

MILLWOOD: 'You're smoking.
I thought you'd given up.'

CHLOE: I changed my mind.
I *can* do that, you know, or hadn't you noticed?
And now I suppose I'll get the silent treatment.
What a surprise.

MILLWOOD: 'I could still make little squeaks.
Tonight had left me that for a sort of injoke.
But I *had* hoped she'd been raped, I mean instead of
you know, lay there and that.'

CHLOE: It's no big deal.

MILLWOOD: 'I must have liked her a tad, because as I say
    I *had* hoped that she'd struggled, but she hadn't.
    No one struggles for me is a thing I'm still
    learning here in zombie class. Where was I.'
    (*TROY gets out of the car and makes to leave.*)
CHLOE: What is this? I mean hello? Where are you going?
TROY: Going? I'm going on. I come and go,
    like anyone.
CHLOE: You can't just – can't just do that,
    do that to me and leave me –
TROY: No one's hurt.
CHLOE: Look what you'll leave me with! You know he hates me.
TROY: Of course he does. I would if I was him.
MILLWOOD: 'He said that and I loved him.
    I hated him but I mean compared to her,
    you see? We were like buddies when he said that.'
TROY: All right, get on the bike. I'll drop you off
    somewhere no one hates you much.
CHLOE: A skid-lid.
    There's no spare. Spare helmet, is there, Troy?
TROY: (*Mimicking.*) 'A skid-lid, there's no spare helmet, Troy...'
    (*TROY grabs CHLOE by the hair and holds her in front of
    ANDRE.*)
    You hear that, Andre? (*To her.*) *What kind of a person are you?*
    Look here's your beau still waiting at his post
    patiently like I told him and here's you
    you come over all practical? What do *you* think,
    old squire? Where'd you fish this charmer up?
MILLWOOD: 'Forgave him everything, I did, I wanted
    to hang out with him, you know, go bowling,
    like with us lads there's nothing can't be forgiven.
    You could tell him that if you liked, it makes no odds.'
TROY: He doesn't know where he found you. I don't think
    he cares. I'm not sure *I* do any more.
    'No spare skid-lid, Troy.' Well if there was,
    you think I'd let you have it? Think I'd sooner

pass it to old Andy. We could burn off
and be a duo, right?

CHLOE: I know he hates me.
He probably always did. I'm sure *you* do.
But how can I stay and face him now? Frankly
I'd rather you killed each other.

TROY: You want some mess.
Some mess for you. No I reckon today I've spilled
more than I meant to on your little half-acre,
sweetheart. I'm off home.
It's not as if my wife ain't waiting for me,
know what I mean?

CHLOE: Your wife? You son-of-a-bitch.

TROY: Gee, howdy, cowgirl. Anyone ever
tell you what you are is drop-dead gorgeous?
So drop dead, gorgeous.

(*TROY goes.*)

CHLOE: Arsehole. Little creep.
(*To ANDRE.*) Don't look at me like that. It's no big deal.
No one'll ever know, unless you tell them,
and you wouldn't want to do that, would you really.
I suppose you need unlocking. Then you'll attack me,
presumably.

MILLWOOD: 'Why would I? I don't need to.
I don't care what you do. You can unlock me.'

CHLOE: Okay. I care.
(*CHLOE releases ANDRE from the pole.*)
Are we going?

MILLWOOD: 'I don't need to.'

CHLOE: Oh, so you'll never leave.

MILLWOOD: 'I'd rather stay here.'

CHLOE: Well I'm not staying.

MILLWOOD: 'That's why I'd rather stay here.'

CHLOE: Secret's out. You really hate me, don't you.
Well. I'd rather stroll to the next town
than watch you feeling sorry for yourself.

MILLWOOD: 'Chloe.'

CHLOE: What.

MILLWOOD: 'Chloe.'

CHLOE: What? What is it?

MILLWOOD: 'You. It's you. You're so stupid.'

CHLOE: Goodbye, Andre.

(*CHLOE goes.*)

MILLWOOD: 'I hope she met the ordinary neighbour
who always kept himself to himself. I hope she
met him on the day he shocked the tiny
community of Piddlebourn. I hope
they get some cracking actress to be Chloe
on Crimewatch in the minutes leading up to.
I hope the viewers realise why he did it.
I hope it's graphic and no one switches over.
Because she knows she's something, and she walks
like that through the world, you know, that coy display
always, how I met her was like that.
"Let's ask this man: can you see my slip through this?"
It's strange to say how sorry I really am not –
not to see her again. You know, it's more like,
you have your turn, your *go* on Chloe, you know?
I did think she was it, you see, I can tell you
now no one's listening.

(*Light up on PAUL.*)

PAUL: And the final one to mention
is Mr Andre Linley, real name Andrew.
He was the only one who did no dancing,
because of being chained to the pole, but then
that was just them and their game. The thing with him was
you couldn't rightly say when he was playing
and when he was being serious. He was always
changing from one to the other without the others,
Chloe and Troy, knowing that he was changing.
That's how things got muddled. It was sad
what happened. You could see it was Mr Andre
things happened to. I saw the ambulance,

I saw him carried in, saw how they nodded
and seemed not in a hurry.
MILLWOOD: 'You see I did think
she was it. At my old age you do, you can't
help it really, you do. If it wasn't *that* one,
it better be *this* one, yes? I –
suppose it was, when all's said and done, it *was* her.
Unless from now I get them all, Monroe
through Cleopatra round to Helen of – well.
Yes. That's how I saw it always anyway.
Beauty coming to Andrew, to Andre. I
wouldn't have settled for less, and I'm glad to point out
I haven't had to, yes. I got in my last
dig at Chloe and anything else she tells you
you'd better be wiring her to the old detector
and watch that needle jump. She is a liar
I came across in the course of things. They what?
"They want to know who stabbed you, Andrew." No one
stabbed me. What I mean is,
"they are not currently looking for anyone else
in connection with this atrocity" – oh sorry,
it's not quite an atrocity, is it, more
an incident, an accident, oh nothing
atrocious happened at all, only Andre,
he wasn't really enjoying it anyway,
life, that green old thing, he was going nowhere.
And I can't tell them. I do know I'd forgot
I had the knife or why I had it – one minute
I'm wondering that and listening to the birds,
(*ANDRE stabs himself.*)
next minute I'm some five foot nearer the earth,
sitting down and calling myself an idiot,
I'm sitting down on the local soil and I'm thinking
honestly did I do that? Because I did that,
and what you presumably want to know is did I
mean to? Let me put it this way, viewers.
I'm the one who had Chloe and very lovely

it was as well, and I'm the one with the motor
that ran out of gas, and I'm the one who let her
go with that thug without a fight and I'm also
him who told you this and it's true, and I'm tired.
And I know something else you none of you know yet.
(*PAUL, with his newspaper bag, runs on to find ANDRE fallen.*)
Somebody saw me do it. You see I cried out,
seeing the blood, and he heard me, whoever he was,
and there he was with a million newspapers,
I remember, they were *Observers*, get it? *Observers*,
(*PAUL runs out.*)
they must have been, and if you locate this chap,
perhaps he can help. Because this case is simple.
I was asking I think a question of myself
or of you all, I thought someone might answer.
And stop me, I suppose, before I asked it.
But no one did. I must have really meant it.
No one else is involved. I am not sorry.
I've come to terms with it, so you mustn't trouble,
and oh I'm *sure* you were *really* going to worry.
But I'm through with love, I assure you. And the next time
you want me, get a model for the voice,
not a frigging dinner-lady, I want a model,
a beautiful blonde one who can hear me talking,
someone to really chat to. Till you do that,
you get the silent treatment. Right. I'm going.
Out through the arched window, to a golf-course.'

Scene Four

(*ANDRE goes; MILLWOOD goes. PAUL reads what he has written.*)

PAUL: 'I didn't want to say it, not use words,
not words aloud, that is, but written words.
Words I'd say would change it, I can't think
exactly how it was and say it. I can though
write it down and hope I do not lose it.
I want to never lose it, it was something
I want to always have, the things I saw.
I mean, before it goes into the past.
Tomorrow it is my paper round again.
I will read about the incident, with the full
names of the three people, there will be pictures,
writing, on page one of every paper
I have. It will not then be part of me
like it is now, that incident I saw.'
(*He crosses all of that out.*)
My name is Paul Castle, aged sixteen.
I live in Cropton and am a school student.
I do my newspaper round on every morning.
On Sunday too, my one day off is Thursday.
I have to deliver newspapers to the three
nearest villages to my village, Cropton.
Between Cropton and Fanfield is four miles
by the main road, but if I ride my bike
along the public footpath when there is no one
it is much less. The only road to cross over
is Fanfield Road, I was standing in the field
nearest there that very early morning.
The reason I stopped there was there was laughing.
I thought it was at me, so I looked round
and saw this sight that made me want to shout
with laughter of my own but made me instead

want to hide, which is what I did. I wish
now I had laughed, but hide is what I did do.
(*Lights down on PAUL, up on the car, as at the beginning:
ANDRE steering, CHLOE pushing.*)
ANDRE: Okay, that'll do.
CHLOE: Girls, this could be yours:
the wheels, the man, the glamour.
ANDRE: Okay, okay,
objective reached. (*He tries the phone.*) No tone.
Absolute zero.
CHLOE: Scoop me off the road
with astonishment.
ANDRE: Been bloody vandalised.
(*ANDRE assaults the phone.*)
CHLOE: That's probably how it happened.
ANDRE: Bloody, bloody hell.
CHLOE: We'll have to hitch.
ANDRE: No bloody chance. Who's going to be driving past
at this time? Who's going to stop?
CHLOE: We could split up,
see who gets picked up first.
ANDRE: That's very amusing,
Chloe, doubly so from the one who decided
to stash my mobile in a canvas bag
in Lincolnshire.
CHLOE: It was safe.
It didn't run out of petrol half-way across
wherever we are – Neptune.
ANDRE: Okay. Options.
CHLOE: Options!
ANDRE: Find a village.
Wait for someone.
CHLOE: Settle here and have triplets.
ANDRE: Good thinking, Chloe. I note intelligent options,
you keep yourself amused.
CHLOE: It keeps me warm.
Have I said crack the shampers open yet?

ANDRE: No.

CHLOE: Well it's coming up.

ANDRE: I look forward to it.

CHLOE: Oh I can't stick empty places. It's so bleak.

ANDRE: It's not what you said before.

CHLOE: I changed my view,
   frankly.

ANDRE: How nice was it seven miles from London?
   You can't see light or houses?

CHLOE: There's a place,
   I went there. Well. I've gone right off the idea.
   They really ought to fill the space with something.
   A little hut with a fire, Andre. Blankets.
   An ice-bucket, why not? That's my civilised
   initiative for outposts.

ANDRE: What I'd build
   on this particular outpost is a signpost
   saying 'ESSO'.

CHLOE: 'M1'.

ANDRE: M anything.
   What do you think are the odds against a whole
   acre of this country being by accident
   overlooked, I mean always, since Domesday
   through Magna Carta, railways, elections,
   I mean always, so by accident there's a place
   existing in the Dark Ages?

CHLOE: The odds?
   Nine zillion to one. But the odds against
   you running out of bloody petrol in it –
   evens, sunshine.

ANDRE: It's possible in theory.
   That soldier in Japan.

CHLOE: Yes that's right, sweetheart,
   console yourself that somewhere on this planet
   someone is feeling a bigger jerk than you are.

ANDRE: You're sounding unhelpful, Chloe.

CHLOE: On second thoughts
   he can survive in jungles, and he thinks

he's still at war, while you won't last a day
without a toothbrush and a trouser-press.
Not to mention a shag.
ANDRE: You mention away,
don't mind me.
CHLOE: Oh pig.
Let's have a drink.
ANDRE: We haven't made a decision.
CHLOE: We pissing have, my darling. You weren't there.
(*CHLOE gets out the champagne with two paper cups. She
passes ANDRE the bottle, she holds the cups. They sit on the
bonnet to drink.*)
To the last Snakecharmers Ball we ever go to.
ANDRE: You say that now in the cold light of day...
CHLOE: Said Chloe then, in the cold light of day.
ANDRE: But you'll be back.
CHLOE: Chloe, who never went back,
sipped her stolen Veuve de Clicquot and thought:
how would they pass the time alone together
in the peasant-inhabited Midlands with no petrol?
ANDRE: This is nice.
CHLOE: I stole it.
ANDRE: I know you stole it.
It's still nice.
CHLOE: It's nicer.
ANDRE: It's the same.
It warms me up, it makes me feel, well...
CHLOE: Makes you feel, full stop. It makes you feel.
ANDRE: What do you feel?
CHLOE: Bee-zarre.
A little bit like – who what when why where.
ANDRE: Right, especially where.
CHLOE: No I don't mind.
Someone has to be here.
Actually no. No one has to be here.
ANDRE: Evidently we do.
CHLOE: There are worse places.

ANDRE: Name one.

CHLOE: ...All right, there aren't. But say for instance
    you're on the sand, say where, say on Mustique,
    but not with me, or this. Is that place worse   (*The drink.*)
    or better?

ANDRE: Easy. Without this it's worse.
    Without you? Oh roughly equal.

CHLOE: Thanks a bunch.

ANDRE: Jesting of course.

CHLOE: I still ought to punish you.

ANDRE: Feel free.

CHLOE: I shall feel free. You won't feel free.

ANDRE: I don't what you mean.

CHLOE: You're going to, though.
    You're going to make a phone-call, Mister.

ANDRE: Oh how?

CHLOE: By walking over there.

ANDRE: It's broken, Ma'am.

CHLOE: But you don't know that any more.

ANDRE: I don't?

CHLOE: You don't. You think it works. You're full of trust.
    Go on.

ANDRE: Where are you going?

CHLOE: Mind your own business.
    (*ANDRE goes to the phone and picks it up. CHLOE goes into the
    car and returns, hiding something. She goes up to ANDRE.*)

CHLOE: Go on then, dial.

ANDRE: Who, though. Who am I calling?

CHLOE: Your vodaphone. You left it in a cloakroom.

ANDRE: *You* left it in a cloakroom.

CHLOE: Not in *this* world.
    (*ANDRE dials. CHLOE brings out a pair of handcuffs and
    chains him to the post. He feigns surprise.*)

ANDRE: What are you doing?

CHLOE: You said feel free, so I did.
    Do you feel free?

ANDRE: No I don't feel free.

CHLOE: I do.

 I'm going over to have a drink. Are you coming?

ANDRE: Oh, maybe not just yet.

CHLOE: You can if you want.

 Just let me know if you change your mind.

ANDRE: I will do.

 (*CHLOE goes back to the bonnet to drink.*)

CHLOE: Shame, this is so nice, this Veuve Clicquot,
 so very nice.

ANDRE: I'm happy where I am.

CHLOE: You're sure? That's good.

ANDRE: Come here, Chloe.

CHLOE: I'm sorry?

ANDRE: Come on, come on.

CHLOE: What is this, a joke?

ANDRE: Come on!

 (*CHLOE progresses slowly, meanderingly, towards ANDRE.*)

CHLOE: Unsure of the man's intentions, little Chloe,
 lightly and filled with trepidation, approached.
 What could he want?

ANDRE: Oh my God.

CHLOE: She didn't know him,
 he could be a monster. He could be in a disguise.
 A prince? A toad? A ssssssnakecharmer?

ANDRE: Oh Chloe…

 (*CHLOE keeps just out of Andre's reach, teasing him. Then he
 manages to catch her and drag him towards her. She struggles
 free.*)

CHLOE: A monster after all. Poor wretched Chloe
 now decided he never deserved to be free.
 She made a big resolve not to let him go,
 where he might pose a threat to the good elves.
 And so, she began her dance of *laisse-moi-seul*,
 or Leave-me-alone, which the ignorant English toad
 would never get.

ANDRE: Oh no, don't dance, don't dance…

(*CHLOE does dance, all around him, out of reach, out of her gown. He sees when we do – and before CHLOE does – the discreet entrance of TROY. Then she sees him too and stops abruptly.*)

CHLOE: Fuck me, it's Easy Rider.

TROY: No don't stop.

CHLOE: Why, have you paid?

TROY: I would. You're a good dancer.

CHLOE: You like dancing?

ANDRE: Embarrassing situation number three hundred and twelve. Get dressed, Chloe.

CHLOE: Why? It's too late now.

ANDRE: And sort this out.

TROY: Sort what out?

ANDRE: It's nothing. It's just –

CHLOE: Oh, I've arrested him.

TROY: Yeah? What's he done?

CHLOE: Tell him, Andre.

ANDRE: Fuck off.

CHLOE: I've arrested him for suspected speeding.

TROY: Very good, Officer. Is this like a summer uniform?

CHLOE: I'm not that, I'm a citizen. Citizen's arrest!

ANDRE: Chloe, not a good idea.

TROY: I'll believe you. Thousands wouldn't.

CHLOE: Where's your little bike? Did you lose it, or fall off it?

TROY: Are you going to dance?

ANDRE: She's not going to dance.

TROY: Oi, you're under arrest.

ANDRE: I'm not. It's only a game.

CHLOE: No you are, Andre.

TROY: He French or what?

CHLOE: He dropped the W.
Or it dropped him. The R and the E are restless,
so soon his name will be *And. And* there'll be no knowing.
ANDRE: Can it Chloe. Don't mind her,
mate. She's sloshed. We went to this event.
TROY: I passed you, didn't you see me? I said: 'Them
they went to that event.'
CHLOE: You didn't pass us.
You hung along like some old hungry seagull
sniffing for fish.
TROY: You got me wrong, young miss.
Sniffing for fizz, more like, that's all I was,
and you're not friendly, sticking out your tongue
like you're this six year-old.
CHLOE: So what are you,
some Knight of the bleeding Road?
ANDRE: Give him a drink,
Chloe.
(*CHLOE passes the bottle to TROY, who drinks.*)
TROY: Piss. So let me get this straight.
You're driving along and you think your bloke is speeding,
so you stop the car and nab him.
CHLOE: Exactly right.
TROY: And chain him to a phone.
CHLOE: It doesn't work.
He knows it's good for him. Don't you, sir?
ANDRE: If you say so, citizen. Good God.
Hands up who's ever been in a situation
more ludicrous than this. That's what I thought.   (*No one.*)
CHLOE: Yes angel, but it's already twice the fun
your Snakecharmers were.
ANDRE: Hey what's he doing?
(*TROY is peering into the car.*)
TROY: Nice motor.
ANDRE: Have it, it's yours.
You can drive it away today.

TROY: I'm checking your tapes.
So we can have a dance.
ANDRE: You can't play tapes,
it runs the battery down.
(*CHLOE comes up to ANDRE.*)
CHLOE: Isn't this wild?
Isn't this sexy?
ANDRE: Nyet.
(*She feels his groin.*)
CHLOE: Here's where you differ.
ANDRE: You mean there's where we differ. I grant it's weird.
CHLOE: It is, it's soaking weird. You need a drink?
ANDRE: I need my head examined.
CHLOE: I need the lav.
ANDRE: Oh perfect. What if I did?
CHLOE: Yes that's fair.
Men have the world to piss in. Women have to
find the nearest forest and form queues.
TROY: Your tapes are dogshit, squire. Put the radio on.
(*CHLOE goes to the car and looks at the tapes.*)
CHLOE: What do you want? Elvis, I suppose.
TROY: You got some Elvis.
ANDRE: Yes, let's all have Elvis.
TROY: Elvis lives.
CHLOE: He probably lives round here.
It's there somewhere. I'm off now on a mission.
If this was a film then you'd never see me again
except in flashback, waving, and you'd say
'That was the last I ever saw of her, Officer...'
(*CHLOE leaves.*)
TROY: Done well, squire. Sensational. Bit nutty.
ANDRE: You know it's all for fun. Our bit of fun.
TROY: You can't have fun with the wife, what can you have?
ANDRE: She's not my wife. I refer to her as my lover.
TROY: I refer to her as fucking drop-dead gorgeous.
You going to marry her?

ANDRE: Oh I don't know.
  We take it as it comes.
TROY: Oh is that right.
  I will if you don't, Andre.
ANDRE: Very droll.
TROY: Was very, wasn't it. Why'd you do it, Andre?
ANDRE: Do what.
TROY: The W. Why d'you drop the W?
  Was it bothering you?
ANDRE: Piss off.
TROY: Come again, Andre?
ANDRE: You heard, piss off.
  As in: that's an old joke, it's getting a tad
  tiresome, so, piss off, said with a yawn,
  not necessarily hostile.
TROY: All right, so it's like what, a pleasantry?
ANDRE: A pleasantry, full marks.
TROY: I think I'm with you.
  I think I'm with you at your event, Andre.
  You're trying to pass the time without your lover.
  I've never met your lover till this morning
  so I never knew I was passing time without her,
  but now I am. And here she is, all finished.
  Cue music.
  (*TROY puts a cassette on as CHLOE reappears. The music is*
  fast. She starts to dance. TROY watches for a while, then joins
  in. CHLOE dances with the chained ANDRE; so does TROY.
  The next track is slow.)
CHLOE: Uh-oh, said she. It's slow, said she.
ANDRE: Chloe.
TROY: I've danced with every dancer hereabouts,
  miss: may you have the pleasure?
CHLOE: Just this once.
ANDRE: Chloe…
CHLOE: I'm having one dance with – who are you?
TROY: Troy.
CHLOE: With Troy, okay?

(*CHLOE and TROY dance. ANDRE, despite himself, is excited.*)

ANDRE: You enjoy yourself.
Then maybe we'll swap.

CHLOE: Yes please.

TROY: Who's going to swap?

CHLOE: You concentrate on dancing, sweetheart.

TROY: 'Sweetheart'!
Slip of the tongue, eh Andy?

ANDRE: Chloe, oh God...

(*After the dance ends, TROY goes into the car. CHLOE goes to ANDRE.*)
Nice dance?

CHLOE: Nice dance. Can I feel? You enjoyed it too.

ANDRE: How far are you taking this?

CHLOE: You feel how far...

(*CHLOE guides his hand between her legs.*)

ANDRE: We don't know what he's like.

CHLOE: We can always guess.

ANDRE: I can't go on, I'm sorry.

CHLOE: You know you can.
There'll never be another time like this one,
will there, angel?

ANDRE: He's in the car. Get him out.

CHLOE: I will, I will...

ANDRE: Do it now, we don't know this guy!

CHLOE: We know the car's not going far. Oi Elvis.

(*CHLOE goes to the car. TROY pulls her in, slamming the door.*)

ANDRE: What? Oh, this is unbelievable.

(*The car window rolls down.*)

CHLOE: Hello, Andre! Look I'm quite all right,
I'm having all our tapes marked out of ten.

(*She disappears again.*)

ANDRE: Get out, Chloe. Oh shit...

(*She reappears.*)

CHLOE: Darling heart! Look, there; nothing happening!

ANDRE: I can see there's nothing happening.

CHLOE: He's just talking.

(*She disappears again, reappearing after ten seconds or so.*)

CHLOE: Hiya!

ANDRE: Hiya.

CHLOE: He's rolling a cigarette!

TROY: I'm rolling a cigarette here, Andy!

ANDRE: You do that.

(*They disappear for longer. CHLOE gets out of the car, smoking.*)

Nothing took a while and a half that time.

CHLOE: It must have been some huge old pile of nothing.

(*TROY gets out of the other car door, as CHLOE reaches ANDRE and gives him a drag of the cigarette.*)

ANDRE: I thought you'd given up.

CHLOE: I thought you had.

ANDRE: Game over, Chloe, okay? Unlock this thing.

CHLOE: Oh. All right. You're not in a mood, are you?

TROY: He's not, is he?

ANDRE: Shut up.

TROY: Oh I think he is.

CHLOE: No he's not. You're not in a mood, are you, Andre?

ANDRE: I'm not. I don't give a shit. I just happened to think there were three of us here, not two.

TROY: What's he on about?

CHLOE: Don't let it keep you awake. You stick to Elvis.

ANDRE: For crying out loud.

CHLOE: You promise you're not in a mood and I'll let you go.

TROY: (*The handcuffs.*) Hey where d'you get these things? they're evil.

ANDRE: Fuck it, I promise, I solemnly promise.

CHLOE: You still in my fan club, angel?

ANDRE: Oh life member.

(*CHLOE frees ANDRE, who goes to the car and looks inside.*)

TROY: Not going to play a tape is he, I hope?

It runs the battery down.

CHLOE: You shut your face.

He's in a mood, after all.

ANDRE: Okay, we're going.

CHLOE: How?

ANDRE: Just going. Put your dress on.

CHLOE: We're lost.

I thought we were going to wait.

ANDRE: No we're not going to wait.

We're going to walk.

TROY: I'd give you a ride but, you know,
only room for the one.

CHLOE: You've no spare skid-lid?

TROY: What do you think, I carry one just in case
I pick up a girl like you? I say, Andre,
where'd you fish this charmer up? I've a woman
waiting for me at home.

CHLOE: You're a son of a bitch.

TROY: Gee ain't that so.

ANDRE: Why don't you make your woman
happy and go home then, pal? We don't need you,
we had some fun but it's over.

(*CHLOE turns away and sits down on the ground. ANDRE,
full of nervous energy and growing suspicion, starts drinking the
champagne.*) You understand that?
We all had a laugh but we're late for where we're going,
so we're not playing. I'm taking my toys away.

TROY: I like your toys, though. Where d'you get those things?

ANDRE: It doesn't matter, they're outs. We love each other
and use them if we want to.

TROY: Marvellous.

Top hole. Jolly good, I say.

ANDRE: I say so too.

Oughtn't you to be going somewhere? It seems
you've taken us for some old friends of yours.

TROY: I say, that wouldn't do.

ANDRE: You go ahead,
you do the funny voice.

TROY: You're taking me
for you, though. Like I do what you tell me to.
ANDRE: I didn't tell you to do anything, pal. I wouldn't.
You're bigger and stronger than me, you probably do
karate or something they give you black belts for.
There isn't a problem here. You go your way,
and we'll go ours.
TROY: I know there isn't a problem.
Grown men and all.
ANDRE: Exactly. Nice to have known you.
(*ANDRE proffers his hand.*)
Andre Linley, thirty-two. In retail.
Chelsea fan for his sins.
TROY: I'm Troy, I'm a hundred.
Support the Villa.
ANDRE: The words 'going' and 'down'
spring to mind.
TROY: Dream on. We beat you wankers.
ANDRE: Everyone beats us wankers. I don't know why
we're still in the league.
TROY: You tell me.
ANDRE: But we are.
It was nice to meet you, Troy. Chloe, we're going.
(*ANDRE goes to CHLOE and finds that she's crying.*)
TROY: What's up with her?
ANDRE: I don't know.
TROY: She's having a good time, doesn't want it to end.
ANDRE: No, I don't think so somehow. What did you do?
You did something, I think.
TROY: Oh come on, Andy,
course I didn't.
ANDRE: I'm not a bloody fool.
TROY: Why don't you chill a notch, as they say?
ANDRE: Fuck you.
TROY: Fuck you, team leader.
ANDRE: Okay okay, relax.
TROY: You fucking relax.

(*ANDRE goes back to CHLOE.*)

ANDRE: Chloe, come on, you're tired.

I'll get you home –

(*Then he realises that all the time CHLOE has been laughing.*)

Look, what the hell is funny?

TROY: There's my girl! He thought you were blubbing!

ANDRE: Chloe!

What are you laughing at? Shut up and tell me!

CHLOE: You, it's you, you're so stupid!

ANDRE: Yes look how stupid!

(*ANDRE hits CHLOE so hard she is knocked down. TROY goes for ANDRE, who turns so abruptly, lashing out, that he fells TROY too.*)

Shit, man, are you okay? I didn't mean –

I'm sorry, I snapped, I meant to –

(*TROY rises to a kneeling position, and draws his knife. CHLOE stirs.*)

Chloe, I'm sorry, I know that goes without saying,

but I am, it's all I've got to say on the matter,

it just, it's all I've got to say – on the matter –

(*He sees TROY's knife.*)

I'm sorry man, I said. I can't help it, you know?

I'm a Chelsea fan! It just happened, Troy, I mean,

how would you feel, I mean, if your woman –

how would you feel if, say, your woman behaved –

you know what I mean –

TROY: Oh yes I know what you mean,

old squire, but I don't have that sort of woman,

not like the matter of this little one you have...

ANDRE: I don't care what went on in there,

I don't care what went on,

I'm saying you'd sort her, wouldn't you, Troy, if, you know,

you'd sort her, wouldn't you, Troy? Wouldn't you have to?

I'm sorry about that – look, are you okay now?

With her, though, look, I did what I had to, you know?

Imagine if she's laughing at you, your woman,

Troy? You're using that knife for a kind of threat?

TROY: A threat, that's right, Andre.

ANDRE: I don't have one.

TROY: No, is that right?

ANDRE: I'm not exactly a fighter.

TROY: Yes you are. We're having a fight, aren't we?

ANDRE: Are we?

TROY: Yes.

ANDRE: It's not a fair one, though.

    (*TROY discards his knife.*)

TROY: What's not fair, Andre?

ANDRE: You're going to kill me.

TROY: No I'm not. But you had a go at me.

    I want a go at you.

ANDRE: There is *no point.*

    (*TROY starts to push ANDRE around. He does nothing.*)

ANDRE: I won't hit back. It'll be a one man fight.

    What fun is that?

TROY: It's lots, you little creep.

ANDRE: Chloe. Police. Ambulance. We are talking

    major pleading here.

TROY: She isn't listening

    any more, Andre, and I'm not either.

    (*TROY tries to fight, but ANDRE won't. Finally he just fells him. CHLOE now has the knife. Neither of the men realises.*)

    You climb in your dream motor and you stay there

    till I'm right out of sight. End of game.

    All over, you little nutters. Where's my knife?

    (*He turns to look for his knife and ANDRE jumps him. They tussle. TROY catches sight of CHLOE as she runs at them with the knife.*)

    The bitch has got it!

ANDRE: Watch it!

    (*TROY and ANDRE dodge the knife and the three of them are locked into a scuffle, in which ANDRE is stabbed. As the three part, he falls.*)

    I'm stabbed. Right there.

CHLOE: What happened?

TROY: He said, you heard him,
    he said, he's hit!

CHLOE: Oh God!

(*CHLOE runs away. ANDRE rests against the pole.*)

ANDRE: She's gone away. Will she get the help I need?

TROY: Yeah, that's right.

ANDRE: Will you stay here to – ah!
    will you stay here to explain?

TROY: No I'll get help.
    I'll – get some help, I will.

(*TROY runs off. His bike roars away.*)

ANDRE: Mm get some help,
    hah! It's not a deep wound, I keep still
    and stop the blood, there, mm.

(*Enter PAUL, with his bag of newspapers. He runs to ANDRE.*)

PAUL: Oh no! Don't worry, I'll go,
    I'll go to the cottage hospital.

ANDRE: Don't go.
    They'll get the help I need.

PAUL: Are you sure they will?

ANDRE: Mm, it's – uh – like a cut, like a shallow cut.

PAUL: It's really bleeding.

ANDRE: Mm, it really…mm-hmm.

(*ANDRE fades. PAUL tries to pull away.*)

PAUL: There's a cottage hospital, Mister Andre.

ANDRE: Andre…
    mm-hmm, Andrew, Andrew…

PAUL: Look it's not far,
    I got my mountain bike!

(*PAUL pulls away and runs for help. ANDRE falters and dies. Sirens, blue light. PAUL goes back to his desk and looks at his statement.*)

'I hope you can read my writing. I would have said it
aloud but that is difficult because things
do not come out with me in a proper order.
Writing is better, because, as well as the facts
I saw this morning I can also add in the things

like how I felt, like I was saying above
how pretty the lady was and how very much
they must have liked her, both of them, Mr Andrew
who cared for her, and Mr Troy with his dancing.
I wish I had stopped them, perhaps if I had shouted
"Stop!" they would not have carried on as they did,
and all of them got safely to their houses.
But it was quite like a dream and I found it hard
to think I could stop a dream in any way.
I expected something beautiful
would be the end of what I saw this morning.
And if I had shouted "stop"
I never would have seen it to the end.
It still seems to be happening in my mind.
I think I shall never forget as long as I live
those three and the strange ways they loved each other.
Signed, P Castle, 9 Beech Street, Cropton.'

BEST MAN SPEECH

Characters

BAILEY, the Best Man

This play was first performed as *The Best Man* on 7 August 2004 at the Smirnoff Underbelly, Edinburgh with the following cast:

BAILEY, Danny Swanson

Director, Jon Croker
Designer, Emily Robinson

Produced by Muse Machine.

Best Man Speech

(*BAILEY is about to give his speech. He has a large wrapped present in front of him.*)

BAILEY: Well. This is the present. Get it? Present.
    I expect you've all had presents
    you'd rather not have had. This is the present
    I've sort of dreaded. This is the present moment.
    And me, well I'm the best man they could find.
    Miranda and Addy. Addy, friend of my youth,
    and I wish you'd leave my youth alone, he's shy,
    and Miranda, blushing bride, only not blushing,
    congratulations, may you – blush forever.
    Blushing best man, it ought to say. It's me
    alone in the present moment, I'm the one
    the light's caught. You can't stop me,
    can you, it's my moment.

    Look at the lovely bridesmaids. Don't they look
    lovely. They're not blushing either. Sammie,
    Jade, and Tabitha. On their behalf
    I answer the toast, I answer the toast. Hey, toast,
    the answer's no. You're going in the toaster.
    That was my first joke.
    (It says here: 'Wait for laughter to die down.')
    Splendid. On we go.

    Now. You're probably wondering about my present,
    my humble offering to the happy couple.
    There's a prize for guessing what's inside. Clue:
    it's a high-tech device for *easy listening.*
    State of the art. I tell you, cutting-edge,
    it'll blow you away, trust me. Now, who am I…
    I should have started there, my mother did.
    My name is Bailey. I do have a first name,
    but they took it at the door. I've got this ticket

to get it back, but till that time, I'm Bailey.
It's simpler for Addy, that, just the one name.
Some of you regulars at this élite
venue, the Maple Vale Country Club,
might know me by my other name of 'Barman,
where's my bloody lager?' or perhaps
'Oi, caddie, that's a friggin' five-iron!' Well,
caddie, barman, waiter,
those are my slave names. But for once I'm here,
in with the cream. I ought
by rights to raise a glass to the supremo
who made the Maple Vale Country Club
what it is today, but as you know,
he happens to be the groom, and he's had enough
compliments for one day, though, having said that,
mostly in his own speech. So I'll merely
thank the staff on duty here today,
(suckers, having to clear up after this lot,
whoops, there goes some more)

(*He throws his drink over his shoulder.*)

and say how very pleased I am to be
among what we always call 'the bastard public'.
(Shouldn't have said that, Addy, should I, no,
looked good on paper.) Anyway, I'm speaking,
I have the floor. Yes, I hear him going,
you'll be mopping it this time tomorrow, Bailey.

Let's talk about today. Today began
for me at dawn, alone on the west beach
at 5 am, *almost* alone, alone
with a drunk unconscious man who suddenly
sat up and said, 'This was a fine idea!'
And here he is, green at the gills and married,
and here am I, who saved him from a fate
even worse than marriage, or at least,
well, neck-and-neck with it. I refer to death.

Look at me. I only gone and done it.
Mention the one thing it says you never
mention in my handbook. Rule One,
the Golden Rule, don't mention it! And now
I'm only drawing attention to it, aren't I?
Look at the present, here, look at the present,
take your mind off death! Now you're thinking,
better stop him speaking, he's not funny,
we feel *un-entertained*. Who is this *Best Man*?

Only his oldest friend. Addy and Bailey.
A to B non-stop, you're there in no time.
But if you know the two of us you'll know
there's really four of us: there's Addy, Bailey,
Croft and Dennis, sure, it's how we met,
Mr Hackett's classroom seating system.
We were all herded into the far corner
at age thirteen, and somehow none of us
ever got over it. Even now, our mates
tend to begin with letters higher than F,
and anyone called Williams or Yates
you shouldn't be in here. It's true. Ask Croft,
he's out there somewhere, Dennis? I can't see him,
he's out there somewhere. Anyway, believe me,
we were the Alpha Boys. Now, chance is chance,
and just some way along from the Alpha Boys
there sat the Alpha Girls, or Alpha Girl.
Ah, he's remembering, he's the blushing groom,
he's thinking: Bailey, don't unwrap the past,
unwrap the present! No sooner said than done!

(*BAILEY unwraps the present to reveal another wrapped
present.*)

Did you hear the music stop? I can never hear
anything but the music stop, and the parcel
always comes to Bailey. Now there's people
staring at me, people I don't know,
and nor do you know me, so you don't know

my sense of humour, you have no idea
if you can step in. And they're filming this,
I see him, I see all of him except
his face, all *he* can see
is mine. If you start saying 'enough's enough'
and wave your arms and barge into my light,
you'll be the high point of this video,
the fool who didn't get the joke! Horror!

The Alpha Girl was Kelly, known to all
as Ashtray. Don't ask why. I think her name
was something like it, but who cares? The Ashtray.
We all know what we mean. The girl who no one
wants around, but then she's always there,
grinning away, all teeth, all lanky hair
and spots and what we're talking is the works.
We're talking your worst nightmare,
except it's ours as it begins with A,
you with me? Here's a story about Addy,
a tale of love and cheating, with a sting,
a revelation, and a true confession…

So we're I don't know, fifteen, and there's this party
A, B, C, D, all the gang, we get there
in Dennis's old man's car, except for Croft,
who rides his brother's moped – this will prove
no mere detail – anyway so we're there,
and girls are there, the girls we wouldn't mind
going a round or two with, so to speak,
and we're playing it cool, we're thinking, as you do,
tonight may be the night.
(Not in Addy's case, I should just mention,
Addy's got form, he's been there, got the T-shirt,
but since Miranda's looking at me again
I won't go into detail. Let's just say,
the rest of us have not got half a T-shirt
to rub together, and those days there was enough
rubbing together going on. For you old folks,

we were all virgins. Down the hatch.) Meanwhile,
the four of us are smoking in the garden,
and then it starts to rain and we leg it in,
and it's like the world just ended. Party's over.
The girl whose house it is has gone. Her parents,
are I don't know, in China.
Probably still there now. So it's deserted.
It's bucketing down, remember, Addy? And Dennis,
we been ribbing him all night, says suddenly
there's someone in the hall, and there she is,
the Ashtray, Kelly Ashtray,
in flesh and bone and about a hundred bangles,
and no one else but her.
And I'm telling you, this house was in the middle,
not in the middle, way out on the borders
of nowhere. People I knew who came from nowhere
had never heard of it.
And the entire frigging caravan had split
to some hot spot, where we were not required,
and the Ashtray's all but naked,
and she's coming on to us, can you believe,
she's making eyes at us, it's a bit too much
for the Alpha Boys.

So Addy and Croft and me
we get in the corner and figure out this plan
that Dennis can make his mark, can post his first
achievement, shall we say, now it sounds crude,
but boys, you know. And then we only hear it,
his daddy's car out there and see the bastard
running up the drive, and our main hope
of rescue's scuppered. Now there's Croft's moped.
'I'm off,' he said, 'and I ain't taking two.'
It's his idea to cut for it, he's got
his deck of porno cards, and it's best of three,
Addy v Bailey, winner rides away
on the back of the bike, loser spends the night
with all that that entails...

Ashtray's in the corner, sort of weirdly
slow dancing with herself, and there's us three
shuffling cards and praying. Addy's gone
to get a beer and when he's out of the room,
Croft, ever a man with a sharp eye
for trading, says: 'I'll rig the deck for you
if you flash me thirty quid.' And he can do it,
I've seen his cardtricks. I could be at home
in half an hour, and all it's going to cost me
is everything I've saved. Not even close.
Now let me tell you, this is news to Addy.
He thought that fate had dealt him a bad hand!
He's going to kill me! Anyway, he comes back,
says he's feeling lucky, and we cut,
and Croft has rigged it and I'm drawing kings
and jacks and poor old Addy
he's slapping down a three. So now, at last,
it can be told! We cheated, Croft and me,
we left you there with Ashtray…
Addy, friend, mate, boss,
your night of love – or as he always tells us,
his night locked in the bog while she was trying
to pick the lock – your night came courtesy
of your best mates, and now it has been told…

This is a Best Man speech. What, did you think
it would be easy listening? Did you think
the news would just stop breaking?

(*BAILEY unwraps the present again to reveal a present wrapped
in the News of the World.*)

Miranda and Addy, come a long way, Addy,
a long way from the middle of nowhere
to sit beside this beauty in her – beauty.
A tale of true romance for all you hardened
cynics in the room: why are we here?
Why are we eating vol-au-vents and little
triangles of salmon when we could be
feet up at home, watching the football? (What's that?

Oh, apparently Croft
is feet up at home watching the football.)
Why are we here? Where did it all begin?
With Four-Play. That's right, Four-Play.
For those of you born yesterday, Four-Play
is a golf term, as in the Four-Play Dance
which is held on the last night of the tournament,
so all the players, you know,
can keep on swinging. So, I'd been caddying
for four days straight for Mr Yamaguchi,
and Addy lets me have these four free tickets.
So I summon up some courage and I ask
my heartache of the time, who shall be nameless,
plus Dennis and someone Dennis
wants to bring. That someone,
as it happens, *is* this bride, Miranda.
Anyway, I book a decent table,
off in the corner, private like. Phone rings,
that afternoon. It's Addy: 'Bailey, help me,
Rob and Geoff are sick, don't let me down, mate.'
And would you believe it, this man here agrees
to work the bar at the Four-Play Dinner Dance.
Born a saint, I was, can't help it. So,
there I am, dispensing alcohol
to the city's premier drunks, do I mean golfers,
while my own table's having a night of it
where I can't see 'em, in the private alcove.
But it did afford me a unique perspective
on love, romance, and matters of the heart.
Or should I call that matters of the liver?

A tale of love and getting 'em in. First out,
waitress brings their order: pint of best,
that's Dennis. Diet coke with ice, my ex,
Chablis, that's classy, must be this Miranda,
and so it goes like that:
pint, coke, Chablis. Pint, coke, Chablis,
every half hour, then it's every twenty,
and I can't see what's happening from the bar,

the waitress just keeps coming,
with pint, coke, chablis. About eleven,
my ex has had enough of gooseberry time,
and gets a taxi home, something about me,
girls just can't get enough, anyway, she's gone,
same ending. Pint and Chablis,
pint and Chablis, and then the order changes,
pint, Chablis, scotch-and-a-twist, aye-aye,
scotch-and-a-twist? Okay,
I know who drinks said beverage: this man,
my mate, I mean, my boss, I mean, the groom.
Next thing I know it's a pint plus vodka chaser,
champagne, scotch-and-a-twist. I read the runes,
I'm Sherlock bleedin Holmes: Dennis is rattled,
he's moved to spirits, she, new girl, Miranda,
has made a friend of Mr Bollinger,
while Addy's keeping steady with his usual.
There's a slow dance at midnight and I see it,
I see it, history made, him and Miranda
in the light of the glitterball and I get a single
order for a *Depth-charge*.
Dennis has lost the plot, he's ordering stupid,
and when the dance is over it's more Bolly,
a magnum for the alcove, one o'clock,
two glasses, two cigars? Two cigars?
That means no hard feelings, that means someone
won and someone didn't. Night wears on.
A limo home for two, then one last order:
one last, lonesome cigar,
and a double brandy, and I'm pouring it
up to the brim for Dennis, my good friend,
when the waitress tells me 'Change that to a bucket,
Bailey, party's over.' There you have it,
correct me if I'm wrong. I did think Dennis
was out there with his lovely…is he not?
He didn't make it, right. You got his name-card,
right, and next to him you'll find his wife's
lovely name-card, lovely. Wrong to talk

behind somebody's back, but he's not here
so where's the harm?
But he'd tell you no hard feelings, and it's true,
that was the night they met, in the Tudor Room
these love-birds of the alcove, I was there,
your correspondent in his Maple Vale
tuxedo and his Maple Vale…cravat
I think you call it.
Anyone care to guess what gift I got them?

(*He unwraps the present to reveal a present wrapped in black.*)

My old mum used to say you can't go wrong
with black. You'll never guess,
or not until too late. Yes I do know,
Sammie and Jade, *I* do know what it is,
it's an easy listening device, did I say that?
It's helping you to listen to my stories.
I mean, we can't help making stories, can we?
Addy, all these business friends of yours
are very still. They want to hear my stories…
And here's a very short one:
BANG! It's a bomb I got in here, do you know that?

So this particular love-chapter closes
with me in philosophical discussion –
eh? Is it really a bomb? What do you think?

The evening ends with me in deep discussion
at 2 am, sloping against the bar,
with Mr Yamaguchi, who decides
my rife has got no rove. I say, 'I'm sorry?'
'Your rife has got no rove, Mister Bairey.'
'I'm sorry, my rife? I don't have a rife,
you have the long man there, Mr Yamaguchi.'
'No! No! Is you, you are the light man, Bairey!'
'The light man, Mr Yamaguchi, no,
I'm the barman.' 'Your rife has got no rove.'
I get him a taxi and he gives me this,
this card he's got, and you may well be asking

'What has this got to do with anything?'
but I may well ask you how can you know
which little arrows point nowhere, and which
are pointing at your head, so sit back,
sit back, Sammie, Jade and Tabitha,
sit back and blush, bride,
sit back, be satisfied,
sit back, Mr Proud-as-punch, sit back,
Mr That's-him-married-off-to-his-own-kind,
Mrs I-will-never-wear-this-hat-again,
Mr and Mrs Cousin-who-don't-like-us,
Old Mrs Have-to-invite-you-because-frankly-
you're-fading, Miss I've-come-here-for-a-husband,
Young Master Life's-a-bitch, and all
you reratives whose rives have got no rove,
and all you businessmen who sit so still,
deciding when THE END will come, sit back
because you don't know what's coming,
and you only ever have to hear this story
once, and then I'm gone, you with me, gentlemen,
ring a bell? You look concerned, gentlemen,
I'll set your mind at rest, in case you're not
entirely sure if it's a bomb or not.

(*He unwraps the present further, to reveal, again, a wrapped
black present, but in the cartoonish shape of a bomb.*)

That put your mind at rest?
Best days of our lives.
Best days of our lives. Always refers
to something long ago. Always refers
to time spent with some people who for years
you made not the slightest effort to keep up with.
Some days they must have been.
Well now you can. Bestdaysofourlives
dot-com. There's a whole website
of everyone you hoped you'd left behind.
'Web' as in a sticky thing you're trapped in.
'Site' as in sore eyes. But it's a godsend

for someone, isn't it, it's a godsend
for a Best Man. A Best Man with the task
of digging dirt on Mr High-achiever…
So. I know my Yahoo from my Google,
and I take a little look into the past,
in bestdaysofourlives.com, and hey,
there they all are, sitting there, the same,
as if they never moved, like some forgotten
weeds somewhere that grew in total darkness
and the light finds them everywhere, remembering,
enormous.

     And I don't want to disturb them,
'cause that would seem like being from the future,
like I'm from Star Trek, and my prime directive
is not to change their world, you follow me?
So I go from site to site,
leave no trace, click, move, double-click,
I'm scanning their depictions of their life-styles,
and they all sound the same, not only that,
they really talk as if those rubbish years
in that shite institution for the stupid
were really the best days they've ever…well,
Latchett, case in point. Peter Latchett,
or 'Thatshit', we were duty-bound to call him,
Latchett was a footballer, a really
talented star prospect, so, of course,
me and Addy phoned him in a deep voice,
said we were football scouts from Upton Park,
wanted to check him out that Saturday.
We go and watch him play, he's looking round
for someone with a clipboard. No one's there,
give him his due, he still plays like it matters,
but no one's there. Point is, it gets a mention.
His message on the website says: 'I once
was scouted out by West Ham Football Club
but now my only contact with the game
is refereeing schoolboys of a morning…'

And of course they've all got children,
somehow, was there time? Was that a class
I missed, perhaps, there's all the school, all naked,
and facing off in two straight lines and me,
I'm smoking in the bike-shed, bingo,
I'm childless, I'm a caddie,
I'll hold your bag, crown prince.

There was this boy called Piper.
Apparently. His message on the website's:
'Anyone remember me?' I spent
a fiver just to join the thing and tell him:
'No, mate, no one does.' He's a family man.
Hope *they* remember him: 'Who's that ugly bloke
in the garden, mum?' 'Search me.'
But I have to join to get my message in:
'Any tales of a disgraceful nature
relating to Mr J M Addison,
warmly accepted,' and I wait around
to see what rolls along. Oh, I forgot,
you also have the option on this site
of pegging up a photo of yourself,
and of the fifty losers from our year
who've joined this club for dead persons, just one
has taken them up on it. You guessed it.
Kelly Ashtray, and I know I said
her name was really Ashtray. It transpires
her name was Kelly *Astey*, well still is,
but bugger me, she puts the thing in brackets,
(*Ashtray*), like she'd better go by that name
or who'll remember her. So there's this photo.
But *it can't be* the Ashtray, it's some woman
made up like a goth and staring out like –
looking at me like she's always looking,
she never bloody stops, and you could say she's
changed, she's lost a bit of weight, okay,
her skin's cleared up, her mouth's shut, anyway,
she's standing in what looks to me
like a crime-scene but may be where she lives,

and there's her little message:
'Any time you're passing Bramble Park,
if you look up my flat's the flat above
the MOBIL sign.' Above the MOBIL sign.
O…kay, I'm glad I know that. Thank you, Ashtray.
Now any time I need a bit of Mobil,
I'll drop by, kill two birds.

Meanwhile: You've Got Mail.
I get some answers. Latchett wants to meet me,
Piper wants to meet me, this Piper
I've never even heard of, saying,
'I see you haven't lost your sense of humour,
Bailey,' and there's Warbeck, who we hated,
a W, you see, that lot were wankers,
and he says: 'Hey, are you the selfsame Bailey
who got a place at the royal acting school,
and said you'd be a star at twenty-five?
Are you related to that bloke called Bailey
who caddies for my dad at Maple Vale?
Maybe I got you muddled.' I can take,
you know, a joke against me, so fair do-s,
I decide I won't meet Warbeck, always was
a loser.

        I meet Latchett.
The most boring night of my life, at least
till I meet Piper, worse. They have no stories.
Addy's their hero, man who made a mint,
man who made himself, not like me,
bloke who caddies, serves, mops. It's a wash-out,
the best days of our lives dot com, I'm going,
I'm disappearing up my origins,
painful, I can tell you.
So I leave the pub while Latchett's in the toilet,
and I'm running down the street, and right on cue
it starts to rain, thank you,
and my hands are in my pockets, and I find
this card I got from Mr Yamaguchi,

with a number scribbled on it. I can hear him,
'You got no rove in your rife, Mister Bairey',
and I don't know if *you* have,
Mrs This and Dr That, but *I* don't,
and something's telling me: this phone number
is just what you would think, it's something dirty,
but another voice is reading it as if I'm
sort of a fool, an innocent like clown,
and this is a number I could use to find
some I dunno, some, *rove.*
So I call it, Sammie. I call the number, Jade,
the man you have returning the gracious toast
on your behalf is a man who calls those numbers,
Tabitha, and it's ringing,
and I'm in a call-box and it's raining hard,
and that's the ledge I'm on. Somebody answers,
I can hear my pulse. Listen. I said listen.
The businessmen would like to hear what's next.
A voice is saying go to Bramble Park.
And I say I will, because it rings a bell,
but I get directions anyway, and the girl
is asking what I'd like. So, I don't know,
so I say, 'I'd like the normal,' it just comes out,
so to speak, 'I'd like the normal style.'
And she says, 'Fine,' she sniffs and says that's fine.
Then I hear her cough and she hangs up.

What, did you think this town was the one town
where no one lived like that? Perhaps you thought
this town the town it never rains,
this town the town nobody's skint,
this town the town nobody's lonely, *ahhh...*
all of them I could have set you right
that evening, had you been there,
all of you who've never had a breath
in common until now... Bramble Park,
a little clump of trees between estates,
and it's raining and it's dark, and by a bench

I see a woman opening an umbrella,
waiting with her back turned,
and I won't waste your time, you know what's coming,
of course it's her, it's Ashtray,
on her soaked patch of earth,
this is her little park, and Yamaguchi's
number is her number.
She isn't skinny, but she's sort of wasted,
white, a little ghostly, and her eyes
made-up and running slightly with the rain,
I notice, and her hair's tied back, but haywire,
nothing's normal. I'm about to run,
I tell you, I been through this film before,
when Ashtray says would I like a cup of tea?
Would I like a cup of tea? I say no thanks
and I suddenly feel I'm falling

and I'm sitting there, I'm saying milk no sugar,
tick-tock, tick-tock,
aren't I, vicar, aren't I, Sammie, I go there,
I visit her little lodging, Kelly Astey,
and it's like I stepped into some old rubbish soap
I'd watched for years. I realise I've always
wondered, had that sort of, had that wonder
about some people, what was it like to be them,
to have spun away somehow,
from, I don't know, the heart of things,
to live your tiny life
with cups of tea and sitting in the park
and making ends meet in the only ways,
how do you get to find those people, Bailey,
I ask myself, where are they, where's the world
that's sad enough to want them? Milk, no sugar,
tick-tock, tick-tock,
Kelly, thanks, I'm sitting here with Ashtray,
I see the rooftops and it's wet and dark
out there, the sun went down but in what city,
is it mine at all, will I see it again? 'I know you,'

she goes, stubbing her fag out, 'you're the one
at school, you were in plays.' 'I was in plays,
true,' I go. 'As that was your ambition,'
she goes, 'I heard you say so in the canteen.'
'What was for lunch?' I can hear myself saying.
'Something we didn't like,' she goes, 'some stew.
I only liked the chips. I didn't like
the stew but when they lifted up the lids
it was always stew. I used to always say,
"When will it be chips?" to Mrs Gladstone,
and she always said it's always chips tomorrow.
That's the law. She was a bit peculiar.'
Hell, I've no idea, I may as well be
on Pluto at this moment, it's so weird,
and I'm staring at the ashtray, no, the ashtray,
and her fingers resting on it,
and talk goes back and forth, talk of great subjects,
stew, chips, but no one's saying much
about the fact I phoned her on that number,
so it's a relief when she lights up, and says:
'I can't do this with mates, if you don't mind.'

And someone's tipped the bowl of the world I live in
and everything's gone awol, 'cause I'm now
some mate of Ashtray's. 'Right,' I say, 'that's, well,
that's sensible.' 'Finish your tea,' she goes,
and I think she's kicking me out and please God,
let her be kicking me out so I can maybe
start my life again, have a bunch of children,
or make a bomb the way I learnt to do
when I was caddying for that old guy
in demolition, he was a class golfer
for someone with no fingers, ring a bell?
He shot an 81 and tried to give me
fifty quid as tip, I said no thank you,
I asked him how you make a bomb. He said
that isn't worth a fiver, and I begged
to differ. Anyway,
'Finish your tea,' she goes, and it's a question,

and I have, and she fills it up and a flaming hour
I'm sitting there as we watch the conversation
die together.

Addy, my dear friend, my old companion,
for you I get the drinks in for the drunkards,
for you I caddie all my afternoons,
for you I sought the dullest of the dull,
for you I was rejected by the freak
nobody ever wanted to go near,
and whiled away the hour with PG Tips
and her old snapshots. Tick-tock. Tick-tock.
Been your Best Man before, is what I'm saying,
long time before I pulled you from the sea
at dawn this morning and just stood there watching
your new lease of life.

Then when I leave, and my resolve is made
to live a different life, somebody else's,
so nothing in the earth will ever bring me
back into this kitchen to sit down
face to face with her,
she says, 'You ought to come again to visit.
Look.' And I say, 'Look at what.' 'Just look,
look,' and so I follow where she's looking,
and there's a bottle there, in a crowd of dusty
bottles on her window-sill:
Bailey's Irish Cream. 'That's your own bottle,'
she says, 'it's got your name on it! I won't
touch it till I see you!' What is it, folks,
the thing that keeps the thing we ought to take
and bin forever – beating in our minds
like it's alive? 'Cause I was back next week,
on a wet Wednesday afternoon we sat there,
sipping Bailey's from an Arsenal mug,
until I'm drunk enough to put my question.
The thing I told myself is the only reason
I'd come back to sit there.

'So, you remember Addison – Addy?'
'Yes.' 'He's getting married. I'm the Best Man.
So I'm collecting stories.' 'True stories?'
she says, she's at the sink, she's washing up,
she's dressed in black, in a long skirt, somehow
she doesn't look too bad, she's got a date,
she tells me, not a customer a date,
but I don't care, I'm sitting with my Bailey's,
having this adventure. 'Right, true stories.'
I'm wondering if she'll bring back that party,
the night of my escape, when we cut cards.
Addy always said he shut himself
in the bog and went to sleep,
while she was outside trying to pick the lock,
so then I'm thinking, what if there's a scoop,
or something Addy never got around
to sharing with us? 'I know something, Bailey,'
she goes, 'and it's so true it's not a story.
I mean, it's got no end. But you're his best man,
so I can't tell you.' 'Who do you think I am,'
I'm pleading, 'it's his wedding, I'm not going to
skewer him on his wedding day.' 'Miranda,'
she says, and I'm surprised, 'is the bride's name.'
I'm wondering why she'd know, and she leans over,
has another sip, and says: 'He told me,
that Japanese.' I say to her, 'I know,
my rife has got no rove,' and she says, 'Bairey,
you've come to the long prace.'

Long prace, wrong place, you see. We had our first
in-joke. Now our time together, our
I don't know, connection had a shape,
had its own flavour, sort of. Its own fravour.
'I'll come to yours on Fliday.'
'What, on Fliday the ereventh?'
You had to be there, Tabitha, Jade, Sammie.
Just old bones to you, you dig us up
it's all you find, yellow bones and in-jokes.
Centuries to come they'll figure out

these two had a religion that involved
this strange sweet fluid. I went back for more,
I drank from my own bottle, my Bailey's,
didn't throw up, I sat there, with Kelly,
passed the time of day, but they weren't times
you lot remember, three o'clock, three-thirty,
Wednesday afternoons, she'd kick me out,
politely but fair's fair. She had a job,
she had 'emproyment'. Said she was a worker.
Said she was on her day off. Then I said
I'm on my lifetime off, my rifetime off.
She grinned like she was grinning through a mask
that wasn't grinning, that was welded on.
Like something lit a candle in her eyes
she wasn't meant to light. A fire-hazard.
Illegal. Like her mind had this one landlord
watching her. This – 'randrord'.

What do we know if no one tells us? Nothing.
All that's there to go by's what we see
done in the world, that's for us or against us.
Stuff was done against her, you could see.
Look at you three bridesmaids.
You can sulk until you turn the colour
someone's dressed you in,
but everybody in your world is *for* you.
Not with Kelly, I could vouch for that,
how much was set against her. Why was I there,
sitting through the silence or the small talk,
remembering such pitiful small details
of stuff so long ago as the tea goes cold,
and the day clouds over, and the sodium lights
come on, all pink, all orange.
Why was I there that long
if I wasn't trying to change the way it looked
to someone, how I'd been? I brought it up,
one day, one day I saw her, all about it,
I said remember me and my two friends,
cutting cards to get away from you?

'But I was ugly in them days,' she goes,
'we were all ugly.' 'We were just boys,' I said,
'we used to have a laugh.' We sat outside,
the time I'm thinking of, the only time
we ever sat outside…
and we're sitting on the patch of ground she shares
with all the other tenants. 'You were boys.'
She was lying on the grass. She said: 'Well well.
Forget it then.' 'Water under the bridge,'
I muttered, like it makes the water flow
faster, cleaner, clearer,
makes it go away, but all it did
was freeze it in our thoughts. She lit a fag.
'Stew under the bridge. You're the Best Man,'
she said, and I somehow first time didn't get it,
I thought it was a compliment, like Bailey,
you're a good man, then I realised my error,
and 'Best Man' sounded like a mockery,
a curse, like being
Judas in a story, so I nodded,
'cause that's who I felt I was, both ways I did,
to Addy, who's my friend, and to, to Kelly,
for being his, his best man. 'If you're Best Man,
do you have to have a stag night?'

Well, you do. Have to have a stag night.
Boy, did we have a stag night. Croft and Dennis,
they could tell you stories, if the bridegroom's
lost for words, or could have if they'd come here,
and Evans too, and Foster, Harris, Latchett,
Mason, Mills, O'Reilly, Piper, Sedley,
Warbeck, Williams, Woods and Yates and all their
heartfelt little messages of *sorry,*
better things to do.

(*He throws many pieces of paper in the air so they flutter down around him.*)

88

But I can tell the stories, I'm here, Addy,
I'm in quite tiptop shape, would you not say,
for someone with two litres of black Smirnoff
in his brains? Boy, did we have a stag night.
And boy, did I do my part, I got the girls in,
I got the strippers in, and a merry time
was had by all, and on to this club, that club,
any club, the six of us, the six
Alphabet Boys, Addy, Bailey, Croft,
Dennis, Evans, and Foster, on the piss,
the Famous Five we were, and you couldn't stop us,
Four Horsemen on the Piss,
the Wild Boys are coming, lock your doors,
they're all expected, all – all three of them,
or is it two these days? The dynamic – couple.
Never trust a barman when you're drinking.
Two litres of black Smirnoff's what it looks like,
but it's only mineral water. I'm an actor,
remember, not your common-or-garden barstaff,
your run-of-the-mill golf caddie, your two-a-penny
garage bomb constructor, I'm an actor
now, like I was that afternoon you told me
if I kept *in* with you, someday I'd have
a hotel of my own, I think you said,
not a caddie shack, or a Maple Vale cravat,
or two weeks holiday or the Wednesday off,
but a hotel of my own. 'Forget it Bailey,
London'll screw you up, the acting game's
a racket, stick around with me, I tell you,
sky's the limit, sunshine.'

Not so lost for words. Mineral water,
mineral water under the bridge. She told me.
If I went to her little flat
with Addy once he'd passed out, on his stag night,
she'd tell me what the secret was, she'd tell me
everything she knew. So I thought, okay,
where's the harm in that? I'll be sober,

I'll give him a ride home when all the rest
have staggered off, he'll pass out, as he does,
and okay, let's see what's up. Let's see a thing
we never knew we'd see.

*(He very carefully removes the outer casing of the joke 'bomb' to
reveal a device with a timer and explosives.)*

The demolition man says don't move.
Simple Simon backs him up: don't move.

Look. She said the story's not a story,
because it's got no ending, but I'm here
today to give it one, and you may hear it
once or never. It depends what's going to happen.
I know there are some among you who, perhaps,
know when a joke's a joke and, what matters more,
know when a joke is not a joke. Some among you
have probably calculated that, on balance,
what you see is what you get. Look.
But you don't know my sense of humour. Or,
it may be the very ones who think they know me
who have that pessimistic outlook. 'Ah,'
they'll say, when they've been rescued, 'always knew
that Bailey for a barstaff.' One of you
in that camp, in that camp with the dark outlook,
has probably been quite gently under the table
tapping 999 into a napkin.
Perhaps you have, perhaps I'll never end
this story. All I ever said of this,
this present that I brought,
was that it was an aid to easy listening,
and if you listen to me, all of you,
table twelve, table five, top table,
we will reach the very end
in one mind, in one piece, together. Now:
what are you scared of? Can you not see him,
Addy, your groom, your relative, your boss,
your ex, your rival, your old sparring partner,

your enemy, your hero,
a little worse for wear but otherwise
alive, saved, still with us? What, did you think
I changed him for a mermaid?

We cut the cards, the bridegroom and I,
one evening all those years ago,
when I was desperate not to be alone
with that ragged hopeful thing,
so I forked out and I cheated,
got clean away and Addy stayed with Ashtray,
the A gang, in a den. And what they did
was to make love, as it's been technically
referred to, what they did was to make love
all night that night, because what he discovered
is why she was despised by all the girls.
*Because there was not anything she wouldn't
do to get some pleasure.* Where we called her
Ashtray, she was known by the cool girls
as Anything. Anything. When the morning came
he'd gone, she was alone in the whole house,
miles from anywhere. She was in love,
she says, but she can't prove it, Anything,
Ashtray, she was alone. The hour came,
the day began, the week began to roll,
and she expected something. She expected
more of what had been... We will one day
be studied closely, human beings, by something,
and it will say in its language: 'These Were Ones
Who Wanted What Had Been.'
We were the Alpha Boys,
we noticed her, we ragged him when we could,
she's looking at you, Addy, and he's stone,
he blanks her in the corridor,
he blanks her at the gate on the way home,
he blanks her,
and then one day he gets her on her own,
and tells her this, she's shoved into a corner

and she's told: 'Yes, we can do the thing we do
when, and only when, I say we do it.
Rest of the time you stay away from me.
Don't follow me, don't mention me, not ever.
Shake on it,' she's shaking, and she does,
she shakes on it, and for about a year
that's how it happens. Addy always says
he's circuit training and he can't be reached,
but he's with Anything in the little hut
along the beach, an hour, whatever the weather,
like the pair in the Swiss clock
stuck on a wheel, you see him when it's sunny,
you see her when it rains, you never see them
in each other's lives,
and this is fine by her,
because he's all there is, and this is all
he has for her. Time passes,
and she leaves school with nothing much to show.
Over the next few years we're all aware
of Addy's star, he makes it, 'sky's the limit,
sunshine', 'can you work this Saturday,
Mr DeMarco needs a caddie', 'sure,
anything, Mr Addison, don't worry…'
and now he's got a share in this and that,
and when it's anything he wants, he knows
a better place to get it. So he tells her,
cut a short story shorter: 'Get lost, Kelly.'
And she tells him, 'Don't leave me.' Well it's not
exactly telling him anything, just saying
'don't leave me', well, it's nothing, it's a prayer,
isn't it, if anything, 'don't leave me'.
A prayer as in unanswerable. And he says,
'If I see your face again I'll have it changed
physically, understand?' And then she's sorry,
she has to show him snapshots that a friend
took for her, she has to say, 'This proves
I love you and you love me,' and he says,
'It doesn't prove a thing,' and she simply says,

'It may be true it doesn't prove a thing,
but I've copies of them in a plastic box
in a local bank. *Don't leave me.*'
He says she's dead. But she's still standing there.
He tries to give her money, draws his wallet
out like a trump card, like his black ace.
But money's not the same to Anything.
And of course he still knows boys, and so one night
he sends the boys round, maybe that will scare her,
and it does scare her. So. That was successful.
Plan A.
But Addy can't just leave her like, let's say,
a bomb, which can go off if she's upset,
or no one's really listening, so he thinks
let's make a deal. You work for me, you keep
a half of what you earn, and you shut up
about us, and I don't
ever have to see you.
That's their deal. She thinks
he doesn't really mean he'll never see her,
so she goes along. It means she can get by.
She gets the businessmen from Maple Vale.
Table eleven know the kind of thing
involved, and there's the boss's Ashtray problem
sorted, they're all happy, semi-happy.
Except the boss is thinking what he needs
is some insurance, something that will make her
thoroughly secure, truly connected.
So the boys go round again, only this time
they bring a nice thing for her, 'Hello Kelly,
want to come to a party?' and she likes
the nice thing they've been working on *so* much
that she wants the thing again, 'When can we do that?'
'How are you fixed tomorrow?' then she needs it,
from time to time, until that time to time
is every day, and then she needs the money,
because the thing burns money,
because the thing burns everything,

though if you saw her, as I did last night,
you'd see the thing's done wonders for her figure.

Which brings us fairly up to date, unless
of course you're watching this on video,
or in another life, in some museum.
The last of the stag boys staggered home to where,
the wife or the television, or to both,
and me and Addy, we were playing the fool
outside the club, except there's only one
fool to play, and which one's playing? He says,
'Let's all go swimming,' and there's no one there
but him and me. I say, 'Let's go for a drive,'
I get him in the back, and he lies down,
and then I drive, we've done this sort of thing
enough that if he's drunk enough he'll fade,
and he's drunk enough.

I get to Bramble Park, it's 4 am
I say he's in the car, asleep. She says,
'We'll take my car as well.' 'You have a car?
I didn't know.' 'Why would you know?' says Kelly,
'we've never had to leave before.' Then I look,
I look behind her, into the flat, and it's all
empty, all that's left is stuff
nobody takes away. 'Where's everything?'
She has this little battered Ford, she has
her life in boxes in it. It's all boxes,
so she can't see behind her.
We're out there in the car-park, and it's clear
she's had it with her life. 'I have a cousin
up north,' she's mentioned her. 'Get in your car
and follow me.' And without really thinking
I could argue this, I could ask exactly why,
I do what Ashtray says. We pull away,
I follow her. And now I know what you know,
sure, I have some trepidation, long word,
Tabitha, I'm scared of what might happen,
because I know she's angry, but a cold –

form of anger, turned cold over years,
and somehow I've just wandered in like magic,
to make her wish come true, but I don't know
exactly what she's aiming for, I just –
know that I'm, I'm somehow, for no reason
I can speak, I'm *for* her, not against her,
and on some level, well,
being *for* a person also seems to
to take away the will-power, not only
take away the breath but take away
the will-power.

We drive down to the beach.
I follow her down there, it's moonless, dark,
there's not a sign of dawn.
I hear her car door slam, then nothing,
then her footsteps crunching across the gravel,
sounds like someone's army.
She gets in, sits beside me,
'My cousin says she'll sort me out,' says Kelly,
'but I ain't seen her since I was thirteen.
She better've changed. I've changed.' I say I've changed,
and she looks at me with nothing.
'We ought to stop at your place, get your things,'
she says. 'Oh, get my things,'
I say by way of answer, 'for the journey.'
And once it's said, it's meant, I'm going with her.
Up north! But I'm still thinking why did she ask me
to bring him here asleep? Now she turns round
'We mustn't wake him up,'
says Kelly, like she's listening to my dream-life.
She holds her hand out to me. When I take it –
and I thought *mine* was cold – I realise
it's the first time we've ever touched. It's brief,
is all it is,
but still, I felt a pull from something so –
so far away it felt like nothing else
had any claim on me.

We opened the back door. He didn't
flinch or say a word. I put my arms
around him from behind and eased him out,
then Kelly took his legs and with our burden
dead to all of it we stumbled down
towards the beach, and we were on the sand.

I started to set him down, now we were there,
but we weren't there, she said, 'Towards the water,'
and chuckling almost at this madness I've
pressed on, and felt the sand becoming harder,
flatter, and she still gave no sign
that here we were to leave him.
Then, about ten yards from where the water's
fingers seemed to reach, she lowered his feet
to the dark sand, and I lowered down his body.

She stood up straight. 'This is what I decided.'
I nodded approvingly, but like play-acting,
because this was insane. 'Do we happen to know
which way the tide is turning?' I said, all
innocent. 'It's coming in,' she said.

She knew. They used to come here.
Her and him. 'This is what I decided.'
'He's dead to the world,' I said, I thought perhaps
the facts required stating: 'He may not be
in any state to save himself.' She started
walking up the beach,
towards the car-park and the lights of town,
slowly, like it was some sunny day
in August, like she had to chart a course
through screaming families, and she a lady
among it all serene, unworried, sorted.
'They'd blame me for it, Kelly, if some sort of
harm came to him, I was his Best Man.'
'You were,' I heard her say, 'but they all know
whatever he says goes, he used to like
to swim on his own at dawn. Didn't you know that?

We swam together once. Only this once
he'd had too much to drink.'
Now I looked back, just quickly.
His arms were by his side,
his face was turned towards us, he was still.
How fast the tide would come I'd no idea,
perhaps he'd wake up at the slightest touch
of the cold sea water. Maybe.
Kelly had reached the car-park,
She had both hands clasped behind her neck,
and was looking way beyond me when I got there.

'Don't want to go away on my own, Bailey.
Need you to read my road map.' My hands
were round her waist, I don't remember
asking them to reach her but they had done,
cupped her on both sides of Kelly's rib-cage
I could feel through wool, and cotton,
flesh and blood. 'I will do,
now what you wanted done's been done.' Then I
looked back to where, quite far away,
the water rushed again, and then receded,
and the small shape lay there. And it occurred
to me it could cost nothing to keep moving,
to fly, it looked so far away, so faint
a thing when all's considered. It couldn't be
that our long years together, all our times,
our wild times, our good years,
even his name, Addison, Addison,
had anything at all to do with that
crumpled length of clothing on the land's edge.

It's just, it's just that very
deliberately I brought my hands away,
raised my forefinger, in a kind of gesture
I meant to mean: 'Whatever I do now,
I'll come away with you, the thing you want
is what I want, whatever I do now…'
and I backed away, and turned and I set out

briskly for the sea. I filled the footsteps
from before, and watched his body grow
from nothing in my sight into a focus,
an object, a monstrous object
of pity. Now the sea
was at him, at his left side, underneath him
a curl of salty sand like a client's arm
assuring him, another round his ankles,
his jacket darkening, his pale trousers
stained while his big empty sleeping head
did nothing. So I got him by his elbows
and dragged him from the tide. I laid him down
and set out for my new life. My new life...

And what do you think I saw, Sammie, Jade,
what do you reckon, Tabitha, as I walked
across the sand towards my new life?
I saw my new life watching me. I saw it
turn from me and get into its car,
I heard its engine start, I saw myself
starting to run and shouting out its name,
I felt myself slowed down, like paralysed
like trying to run in dreams,
then I saw it drive away,
and I stopped dead in the sand,
this morning, without it.

And I wanted to let you know that there is nothing,
nothing after all...

(*He cuts the wires attached to the 'bomb' and confetti showers
out.*)

left of my new life. You can relax,
Death didn't turn up either. This is my present.
To Addy, *your* life,
to Miranda, *his* life,
and to the rest of you, whatever lives
you lead in your glad rags. This is a toast
to a girl you never knew

and will never see and who I won't see again,
which is all I share with you. Please don't forget,
when you come to rub me off this video
or file away this time,
that a fine way to remember things forever
is to wish they'd never been.

(*He leaves.*)

(*Fade to darkness.*)

THE LAST VALENTINE

Characters

LUCE
who tells the story

JAZ and MISH
her girlfriends

CABB, FOSS and HUTCH
the boys

RAY
the new boy

This play was first performed in October 2000 in schools in North London and at the Almeida Theatre, with the following cast:

LUCE, Nadine Marshall
JAZ, Cathy Owen
MISH, Nicola Harrison
CABB, Jonathan McGuinness
FOSS, Charles Baker
HUTCH, Alexander Newland
RAY, Simon Walter

Director, Ben Harrison

Produced by the Almeida Theatre.

The Last Valentine was written during the Performing Arts Lab held at Bore Place, Kent in February 1996. The author would like to acknowledge gratefully the help of the writers and teachers who were with him on that course.

The Last Valentine

(There is a bench, and a space elsewhere for the six friends.
LUCE comes. She addresses the audience, in the voice of
Heidi, a rich girl.)

LUCE: You all have friends. I can see them. What you can see
    is Heidi, me, my friend, but she has no friends
    (Her voice changes.) or Lucy, me, like this and she lost her friends
    one by one on the night of Valentine's Day,
    the last one, then. Maybe you sent one or got one,
    so you remember hoping or wondering
    something maybe. But me I lost my friends
    that night, or the five I had,
    the five I liked. If you have five you like,
    now think of them all gone away, and remember Lucy
    like this – or Heidi like this – next Valentine's Day.
    (JAZ and MISH come.)
JAZ: What I really hate is January, 'cause whatever
    you do at Christmas –
MISH: It's Christmas I really hate –
JAZ: It's Christmas, but when it's gone you have nothing ever
    till summer –
MISH: Summer's okay if you like summer –
JAZ: Can't bear it, get hay fever –
LUCE: You do get Easter –
MISH: You do but not till then and it's always ages,
    Luce, till then, or it is in January ages.
LUCE: *(To us.)* We were bored as anything but we knew this boy,
    or rather, we didn't know him. We knew his name.
JAZ: *Roy*, who's that?
MISH: I know him, the guy who's leaving.
LUCE: Not *Roy, Ray.*
MISH: Who's Ray, is he leaving?
LUCE: No,
    he's staying, the one who's new.

JAZ: Roy isn't new,
   he's been here ages.
MISH: I said, that's why he's leaving.
   He's been here ages.
JAZ: Everyone's been here ages.
LUCE: Ray, I'm talking about! (*To us.*) We knew this boy,
   and there was, you know sometimes there's something
   it sort of *gets* you about someone. It's not
   anything much you can focus on, but you know,
   it bothers you, it was better before he came,
   or she came or it came, whatever, but this was a boy,
   he was new and his name was Ray.
   (*CABB, FOSS and HUTCH come.*)
CABB: I know who she means.
FOSS: Search me if I follow you.
CABB: It's Ray she means.
HUTCH: I hate him, if you want I'll tell you why.
FOSS: You hate everyone, Hutch.
LUCE: (*To us.*)   The boys we knew
   were just the same as us, it was like we caught it,
   part of us being friends, it was, though I know
   I know it was me who started it with Ray.
CABB: I hate his attitude, it's like he's better –
   he's not. I'm saying he's not, but it's like he's saying
   he is, he's better –
HUTCH: He said he's better? I hate him.
CABB: Not in so many words, he didn't.
HUTCH: That's him, though,
   hiding stuff, like he does.
MISH: Who cares, he's leaving.
JAZ: That's Roy, not Ray, who's leaving.
HUTCH: Is Roy leaving?
   Good, I *hate* him. Ray, I mean.
LUCE: I don't hate him.
CABB: I don't hate him either, Luce,
   it's his attitude I'm emphasizing.
FOSS: I like him.

MISH: You *like* him? You like Ray? He likes Ray.
    Hey Jaz, Foss likes Ray!
FOSS: I got you, Mish!
    I got you mainstream there!
JAZ: I didn't buy it.
FOSS: Can *I* get a word in though? He never laughs.
HUTCH: He's laughing at us inside.
FOSS: He only smiles.
    He only smiles, like, I do a gag, and you lot,
    you crease or whatever, you know?
CABB: Sure, you're so funny,
    Foss, you fold me up.
FOSS: I have in the past,
    done that, Cabb, like you say, whatever, folding.
HUTCH: He's killing himself inside.
FOSS: But Ray, I'm saying,
    just only smiles, you know, like Cabb was saying,
    he thinks he's better.
JAZ: I don't care what he thinks
    of Foss and his sad old jokes, what I can't bear
    is how he's always staring at us.
LUCE: He's not
    always but you're right.
MISH: She is, she's right,
    Jaz, you're right, I've seen him always staring.
    He's always staring at me sometimes and sometimes
    he's always staring at everyone.
FOSS: And smiling,
    smiling while he does that staring.
MISH: I never
    said what it is with me. With me it's this
    gentleman thing. He's saying like I'm a girl –
JAZ: You are a girl.
MISH: But he's making it clear, Jaz,
    letting you go ahead in the queue, or like
    holding open the door, I hate that. I bet
    he'd put his coat in a puddle, like that lady

so Nelson wouldn't get his shoes wet, you know?
in History that time.

HUTCH: He really did that?

MISH: Nelson, yeah, 'cause he couldn't see the puddle.

FOSS: Not Nelson, Ray did that.

HUTCH: That's why I hate him.

LUCE: It's not that I *hate* Ray –

CABB: What really gets me
is people talking about him. For example
'Ray did this,' or, you know,
'Ray did that,' and it's girls who do it, it's like
what I'm saying is 'So what? So what if he did?'
but you don't hear girls saying ever
'*Cabb* did this or that,' and reacting to it,
discussing it or whatever, mulling it over
in morning break.

FOSS: He's right, and you never either
get anyone saying 'What's *Foss* been up to lately?'
although there's loads I could say if it did come up.

CABB: So what if Ray did this?

FOSS: So what? You're right,
let's let it rest, that topic, the Ray topic,
'cause, Cabb, you're right, he's right, so what?

JAZ: And those boys
they're always on about him like he's some
major deal when he's not, he's minor.

MISH: He is,
he's minor, Ray but he's staring at us always,
as if we care he's doing that, or we're thinking
'Why is he always doing that?' which we never.

LUCE: I never said I hated him.

HUTCH: I did,
but in case you missed it I'll slide it by again.
I hate Roy.

LUCE: It's Ray.

HUTCH: Oh yeah? I hate that,
'cause who does he think he is? And I meant to add

it's a free country, so I can hate who I hate
and keep my reasons classified.
LUCE: I never –
(*To us.*) I never said I hated him. In a way
I didn't hate him at all, like I even felt
feeling for him, I mean, with wondering sort of
who he *was* exactly, because he just came
out of the blue in the winter term, and we couldn't
place the way he looked or the way he talked,
the rare times he was asked and would have to answer.
There was nothing, I mean to *go on* with this Ray,
nothing at all to go on. So one day,
not Valentine's but before, in the weeks before,
with Christmas moving away and instead of it getting
lighter, it getting colder and darker, one day
I wrote to him, to – Ray, can't say why I did it,
I didn't say who I was, or rather I did say
but what I said was I was
Heidi, I don't know why, and I said I lived
in a mansion in a great park, that I had horses
and I'm not like that at all, I never liked horses
but Heidi did, still does, and she sat in the hall
of a high white brick mansion
with pillars on the outside
at the end of a beautiful lawn and we had a pool
I told him – not that first time, that was later –
I only said I'd seen him once, down the shops,
and I wanted to be his friend. My name was Heidi.
The Friday night I posted it in the dark,
Jaz and Mish came round and I did try
not to, I mean, I did try to hold it in,
my new identity, Heidi the lonely rich girl,
sad and forlorn she sits at an upstairs window,
writing to Ray in her green ink on her special
crinkly Christmas writing paper – but then
I was miffed with them always yacking about themselves
and thinking, 'Oh she'll just listen, oh yeah Lucy,

she'll just listen and laugh!' So I did tell them.
(*JAZ and MISH shriek with laughter.*)
That in a matter of hours when we next woke up,
that Ray, he'd have a new love in his life!
JAZ: New? First one ever, you have to be meaning…
MISH: He probably thinks you want to go bike riding
    or train collecting or what!
JAZ: This is solid funny.
    It's almost cheered me up.
LUCE: (*To us.*)   She cheered *me* up,
    Jaz, she was always sighing, I'd always think
    at least I'm not that miserable.
MISH: What you do,
    is say you're the only child of the dynasty,
    last of the line and they want to marry you off
    to royalty but you'd rather –
    (*They all laugh.*)
MISH: – You'd rather write to Ray!
JAZ: Are you going to get him
    writing to you?
MISH: Oh you must!
LUCE: No, I couldn't, I'd have to
    say where I lived –
MISH: No you don't, you can tell him to leave
    letters in trees or something, holes in the ground,
    under the carpet – why don't you tell him your dad's
    this wicked evil man and he's locked you in
    with bread and water and that, and you've never seen
    the outer world!
LUCE: I said I saw Ray in the shops –
MISH: In a crystal ball in the shops, you could say, like a dream,
    and only he can wake you up with a kiss
    like Cinderella, you know and the Beast?
LUCE: I could say
    I'll jump from the roof of the mansion unless Ray –
MISH: Ray, unless Ray –

LUCE: Unless Ray rides up on his charger
   and fights my dad to the death!
MISH: G'on, write it down.
JAZ: No, do stuff he believes.
MISH: What fun is that?
JAZ: It's all the fun there is – he'll think this Heidi
   she's real, she really likes him.
LUCE: Heidi does
   really like him. I mean, in Heidi's world
   Ray's the greatest.
JAZ: Do stuff he believes.
MISH: Yeah, but have some evil, like some danger,
   then he'll believe he can help you out or something.
JAZ: Yeah Ray can save the day.
LUCE: (*To us*.)   It went on like that.
   Every Friday they came and we had ideas,
   what Heidi was up to next, where she went riding,
   how things from China, she liked, she was always getting
   gifts from there, her father was always doing
   government secret stuff, and how every day
   she picked her way across a meadow of snowdrops
   to get to school! We could all imagine him out there
   asking about this field like there truly was one,
   when it was only Heidi's world. We did that,
   every Friday, the story, and then I wrote it
   and posted it. He'd have it on the Monday,
   to start the week. And you could think that's cruel,
   and maybe yes but you'd see him walking along,
   he never smiled any less, and he still did things
   like holding open the door, and he worked hard,
   did well in tests, it's not like he wasn't happy,
   Ray, and he stared at everyone just the same,
   like it was always new to him, and the times,
   the rare times he was asked, he would always answer
   questions in his quiet tone, and we thought
   we'd help him, because we'd make him
   think there was someone about who really, like,

who loves him, you know, a lot, so it didn't matter
there wasn't. I mean anyone in the world.
It ought to have ended there, with Heidi's stories.
She really did mean no harm, but it went further.
CABB: Jaz and Mish are saying they write this letter,
every week, at Luce's place, I think Luce
is in on it and they do it and send it to him.
FOSS: *He* wouldn't get the gag, though, he'd only smile.
HUTCH: I bet he knows it's them.
That's typical of him, he's always snooping,
on the prowl.
FOSS: And what does he write back?
CABB: To them? He doesn't.
HUTCH: Bastard, letting 'em stew.
CABB: He doesn't know where they're coming from.
HUTCH: Oh, I'll bet.
He knows more than I'm saying.
LUCE: (*To us.*)   That wasn't my fault.
The lads, I mean. That was Jaz and Mish. It was just
they showed up once on the Friday, we were a bit
giggly I think and I can't remember who said –
ALL: LET'S MAKE A DATE.
LUCE: Let's make a date, like a blind one, get him to come
and wait somewhere, for Heidi –
ALL: SEE IF HE DOES IT.
LUCE: See if he does that, really believes in her, wants
to see her close up, like face to face, on a date,
because soon it's Valentine's Day –
MISH: If he comes that day
we'll know it's love!
LUCE: But he knows our faces.
JAZ: Sure,
but we won't show. I mean, there *is* no Heidi,
it's just to see if he comes –
BOYS: YOU COULD TELEPHONE.
JAZ: Yes, he won't know your voice!
MISH: He'd never know you!

LUCE: Why me?

JAZ: Of course it's you, you began it, Luce,
      you're Heidi, after all.

LUCE: Nobody's Heidi.
      (*RAY comes to the bench. He has some flowers, a magazine, and
      a jacket with some orange in it.*)

JAZ: Oh phone him, Luce.

CABB: Have a drink.

MISH: Have a drink.

JAZ: Oh phone him,
      imagine his face – she called me, she really means it,
      there's really a house and a lawn and a field of snowdrops!
      I'll be invited there!

MISH: It's a blind date
      with his dearest friend!

FOSS: But you gotta think of where,
      so we can watch, you know? 'Evening, Ray,
      seen any good films lately?' sort of thing,
      show him, you know, we saw you.

CABB: No, you'd blow it,
      Foss, you'd crease.

FOSS: I'd never!

HUTCH: I would *inside*,
      getting him back like that.

FOSS: Getting him mainstream.

LUCE: But listen, it's like –

CABB: You have to do this, Luce,
      it's memorable.

JAZ: It's mega-memorable.

CABB: Drink?

LUCE: It's like it would end it, though, if he didn't come,
      and if he *did* it would end it, 'cause then he'd know,
      he'd know there was never a Heidi –

MISH: He ought to know,
      I mean, at his age or what.

FOSS: He's like deluded,
      innit? Can't be good for the guy.

HUTCH: It's time
    he stopped the nonsense, lived in the real world,
    learnt the hard way.
JAZ: It helps him in the long run,
    the longer term.
ALL: YOU GOT TO PHONE HIM, LUCE.
LUCE: So I did phone him, I did,
    early evening Saturday, I was nervous,
    I had a pain low down like an indigestion
    and Jaz and Mish were there.
JAZ: Is he there?
LUCE: Be quiet,
    it's ringing!
MISH: It's ringing, oh God!
LUCE: Shut up! (*To us.*) I had to
    keep my wits, it was Jaz and Mish who were like
    wetting themselves and it wasn't them who were phoning!
    I remember thinking – I'm Heidi,
    I live in a great white house on a hill, I can see
    from here while I'm talking, fountains and stone dolphins,
    marble dolphins – further away there's a forest,
    the sun's going down (I'm thinking in case he asks me)
    but Jaz and Mish keep giggling – you've got to be quiet!
    (*To us.*) Then suddenly he was there and he didn't ask me
    much at all, not anything I remember,
    but –
RAY: Will you be there?
LUCE: Of course, it's a date – I said,
    'a date' but while I was saying the word I was thinking
    'There's a date there'll never be, not the fourteenth
    the forty-fourth of February.' – Of course,
    it's a date.
RAY: Then I'll be there.
LUCE: He goes. 'Do you promise?'
    I asked him, I hadn't planned to,
RAY: Yes, I do promise,
    Heidi, and do you promise?

LUCE: It was sort of lucky
    he called me Heidi because, if he'd called me Lucy
    and asked 'do I promise'… But he did call me Heidi,
    and I saw the lawn and the fountains and all around
    the silver spouting water and I did promise
    I'll be there, Ray, of course, I promise. – It was then
    the lads came round again, and it wasn't my fault
    the things they started saying.

CABB: Flowers, Heidi,
    flowers or you're not coming.

RAY: Do you like roses?

LUCE: (*To the others.*) Do I like roses?

JAZ: You bathe in roses.

FOSS: Orange,
    that's your favorite colour, they got to be orange.

RAY: They're not in season, Heidi.

LUCE: (*To the others.*)   They're not in season.
    (*To RAY.*) Plastic's fine, lasts longer! But I like orange.

RAY: I know you do.

LUCE: (*To the others.*) He knows I do.

FOSS: Yeah, and tell him,
    he's gotta wear stuff that's orange, something orange.

MISH: Yuck.

LUCE: (*To RAY.*) Like a scarf?

RAY: I can lay my hands on a jacket
    with orange in it.

HUTCH: And he better be holding a copy
    of something, shows he is who he *says* he is, right?
    Else you can't trust him.

JAZ: How about *Hello*?

HUTCH: *Men Only*!

FOSS: *Sunday Sport*!

MISH: *Just Seventeen*!

ALL: *JUST SEVENTEEN*!!!

LUCE: (*To RAY.*)   *Just Seventeen*, and the time?
    Eight, I promise.

RAY: I promise as well.
LUCE: And you promise
    to wait for me?
RAY: I promise.
LUCE: Well it was Tuesday,
    Valentine's, and we all met at mine to start with,
    because it's near this field where there's this bench
    with an old man's name on it, it's carved, like he left it
    to us in the town and hundreds of scratched-on names
    of lads and girls they like but are much too scared.
    It's where we said to go to. It was wet,
    not raining now but dull, we watched from about
    twenty yards…? I don't know, from behind a wall
    of a garden we climbed into, and he was there
    at ten to eight with everything, he was there!
    The game was won, he'd fallen for it! Only,
    here he was, the real Ray, still falling.
CABB: Wipes the smile.
JAZ: Big time.
FOSS: Gag's on him now.
MISH: We're doing the staring.
HUTCH: See, he can't take it.
LUCE: (*To us.*)   And yes,
    I felt it was over then, my game of Heidi,
    because he'd know, and he'd wait maybe half an hour,
    and wander away. You could think we were cruel people,
    you could, because I did but I didn't say so.
    Something hurt. It was fountains,
    sunset, dolphins, a horse and a field of snowdrops,
    it was losing them for the first time.
JAZ: I'm cold.
    I'm thinking toast, I'm thinking *cappuccino*,
    MTV…
CABB: How long's he been there?
FOSS: Hours,
    months.
CABB: Who's got a watch?
JAZ: Forty-five minutes.

FOSS: Oh what, that's got to do.

CABB: Let's call it an hour.

FOSS: That's sweet, Cabb, that's major of you, that is.
     I hope he's grateful, stupid git.

JAZ: I'm thinking
     video, I'm thinking chocolate, Luce,
     let's knock it in the head.

LUCE: I'll stay till nine.

FOSS: I hope he knows you care.

LUCE: (*To us.*)   But when nine came,
     Cabb seemed to change his mind, he started nodding…

CABB: Look. I can't believe he hasn't gone yet,
     but there it is. I don't care if you're with me,
     I'm going to tell him –

LUCE: No!

CABB: I'm going to tell him
     it isn't safe around here, that's all. I know
     he's new so he wouldn't know one way or another,
     but that's what I want to do. That, is my action,
     then I'm off home. It's worked, I think we agree,
     we're satisfied, but I think we owe him something
     for sitting there, okay?

LUCE: (*To us.*)   Nobody argued.
     I think we were all annoyed by Cabb, for being
     well, the one who thought of that, but glad,
     that someone had, that someone would put an end.
     He walked towards the bench.
     (*CABB approaches RAY.*)

CABB: It isn't Ray,
     is it?

RAY: Yes, that's me.

CABB: You know, it's Cabb
     from school. I thought I recognised you. Nice,
     nice jacket, Ray, what's that you're reading?

RAY: Well,
     Just Seventeen.

CABB: That's excellent.

RAY: It's not,
   not really, I'm just holding it for a girl.
CABB: A girl?
RAY: That's right, who asked me to.
CABB: That's, well,
   excellent, that is... Look Ray, can I tell you
   there's trouble here most nights and I'm just passing
   by, you see, and I reckoned you wouldn't know,
   you being new to the neighbourhood, you see,
   you wouldn't know how it gets.
RAY: It seems quite quiet.
CABB: It always does. It's then when it's dangerous, Ray.
RAY: I've not seen anybody. The girl's quite late,
   so I haven't seen her either.
CABB: Well... She knows,
   you see, I mean, she knows there's trouble here,
   Ray, so she's not, it's possible, not coming.
RAY: She promised to.
CABB: She – right.
   Okay then, Ray, fair do-s, it's just a warning
   really, about the dangers. Usually now
   it starts, around nine, the trouble –
RAY: It's quarter past.
CABB: Or – ten, sometimes, it's equally often ten
   it starts and it's awful, Ray.
RAY: Cheers. For that tip-off.
CABB: Right. Don't mention it. Major flowers. Sweet colour.
   (*CABB returns to the friends, defeated for now.*)
LUCE: So Cabb came back with a shrug but he didn't go
   like he said he would. He lit up a cigarette
   and bet us a crate of beer we couldn't do better.
   (*HUTCH takes up the challenge, and faking panic, approaches*
   RAY.)
HUTCH: Ray, my man – I can't believe you're here –
   you've got to save me, man, the pigs are coming –
   I'm finished. Look, I've had it, take these pills,
   stash 'em, man, they ask you, you say nothin',

'cause if you grass you're dead meat, you got that?
(*HUTCH runs off back to the gang.*)
He'll split for sure, he'll cack it.

CABB: We're waiting.

JAZ: Looks like he's staying put.

HUTCH: The pigs'll kill him,
they find that shit on him.

JAZ: Well they might kill him
if you hadn't just invented them.

HUTCH: That man
is seriously dead.

JAZ: Or perhaps he knows
he's not in a cop movie.

CABB: It's not working.

FOSS: That's 'cause it's not subtle. Me and Mish
we've cracked it, we're a team.

MISH: He's not my boyfriend
but we made a plan together.

FOSS: Yeah and it's subtle.
We walk up there, and then – what is it, Mish,
the subtle section?

MISH: We're going to mention Heidi,
but like she's someone somewhere else, you see,
with loads of blokes, so he's just one of many,
one of a load, so it's not like she's like no one,
she's someone but a bit of a goer, you know,
like Marion Munro in that film she's in.

LUCE: (*To us.*) So off they went and what could I do to stop them?
I started this, this Heidi. Their new Heidi
was nothing like the kind of girl in the letters.
They went to work and I watched and I couldn't stop them.
(*MISH and FOSS approach RAY.*)

RAY: You're not the pigs.

FOSS: Say what?

RAY: A friend from school,
the pigs were chasing him so he left his tablets.
So here they are if you meet him.

MISH: That'll be Hutch.
  Er – probably –
FOSS: Or – possibly –
MISH: And he's not
  quite with us.
FOSS: He's nowhere near us!
MISH: I mean,
  he's not quite on the planet.
RAY: Yes, I thought that.
  Another boy said it was rough here,
  but it seems quite quiet, pleasant even, but cold.
FOSS: Freezing, innit? Freezing...
  Freezing. Woo. Burr!
MISH: (*To FOSS.*)   'Burr'?
FOSS: (*To MISH.*) Yeah, brr, brr...
MISH: Oh, brrr...
FOSS: Look matey,
  do you mind very much if I ask you what you're up to
  at half past nine on Tuesday night in a field?
  You been here hours.
MISH: (*To FOSS.*)   We don't know that, tosser.
FOSS: You been here
  possibly hours and you show no sign of leaving.
MISH: You don't have to tell us anything at all,
  Ray, is it? Don't mind my friend, he's not
  my boyfriend, but he's all right.
FOSS: Who said I want to
  be your boyfriend?
MISH: No one, I'm just saying,
  you're not. Because if you were,
  I'd be two-timing you and Barry (my boyfriend)
  and that'd be just like Tezza Moss with Amber
  and Kylie Churchill, or, even worse, like *Heidi...*
  Heidi and all her blokes...
FOSS: Oh yeah very like Heidi
  that would be...

RAY: It's odd that you mention Heidi,
but *I'm* waiting for a girl named Heidi.
MISH: It *is*,
it is that Heidi, there's only one.
RAY: One Heidi?
MISH: Yeah, I remember someone saying it's odd,
but she's the only one in town.
RAY: This Heidi
doesn't live in town.
FOSS: Only one in the county.
RAY: She lives I think in a county with more hills
and woods than this.
FOSS: Only one in the world, one Heidi.
MISH: (*To FOSS.*) You dickhead, Foss.
FOSS: One Heidi, seven boyfriends.
Wasting your time, old son.
RAY: Oh I don't think so.
MISH: The Heidi we know is rich and she's got horses.
RAY: Absolutely, that's her, but I didn't know
there's only one with the name.
FOSS: Loads you don't know.
RAY: You're right, but you could help.
For instance, what does she look like?
FOSS: ⎫ ⎰   Blonde.
MISH: ⎭ ⎱   Dark.
Er, blondish-dark, like a blend, you know…
RAY: Yes, I know her,
through letters, though, that's all. Blondish-dark…
MISH: Yeah, she's okay, but it's like, I ought to tell you –
letters to everyone, Ray.
FOSS: It's like an illness,
a syndrome, Ray, a fatal syndrome.
RAY: We talked,
on the phone, we fixed a date. She promised.
FOSS: She promised.
All right, you see that moon? I headed that

up in the sky, I did, and that's a promise.
See? I promised.
RAY: A different kind of promise.
FOSS: (*To MISH.*) I'm losing this. He's nuts.
RAY: Anyway, *I* promised.
I promised to wait. And I'm here, so that came true.
FOSS: You wanna know what else?
MISH: (*To FOSS.*)   Don't tell him, Foss.
FOSS: Loads that he don't know.
MISH: We're going, goodbye,
Ray, whatever, goodbye.
RAY: And you be careful,
the trouble might start late tonight, it starts
at ten as often as nine, and it's sometimes awful.
(*FOSS and MISH rejoin the friends.*)
JAZ: He what?
MISH: He's there because he promised.
CABB: Because he promised?
What century are we in?
LUCE: But he did promise,
and so did I.
CABB: You did not. Heidi promised.
MISH: She did, the stupid girl, and now we're all
suffering.
HUTCH: I'm not suffering.
FOSS: Me neither.
You suffering, Cabb?
CABB: No way, I'm going to sort this,
Jaz and me, we'll crack it. Go on, Jaz.
JAZ: You watching carefully, children? How to make
a squirrel leave his perch.
HUTCH: You shoot him off it!
JAZ: You show him something better…
(*CABB and JAZ approach RAY.*)
LUCE: (*To us.*) And off they went. Foss and Hutch and Mish,
I felt them looking at me, though when I looked
they weren't, they were looking at them, but I couldn't help

feeling they were thinking
now it was me, the only one who hadn't
thought of something yet. All I'd thought of
was Heidi, who she was, the times she walked
in the ornamental gardens, by the sundial
in the peach and damson dress, or wrote her diary
up on the window-sill so you could see her
face between the flowers. I hadn't thought of
how to bring her here. All there was here was
more and more of this lying, and all the time
they lied I thought of Heidi and I even
I even thought of Ray not there where he was,
but standing near the fountains, looking up,
looking up at the windows, looking down
at his silver invitation card and smiling,
but of all that I was thinking,
only the smile was true yet.

CABB: Howdy, Ray.
You're a braver man than I am.

RAY: I don't think so.
You're here as well, in the danger area.

CABB: Sure,
but they know me, they've done me in three times
so I'm no fun for them.

RAY: They've done you in?

CABB: I'm used to it by now.

RAY: There's still no sign.
Just two more from the school. They got a bit muddled.

CABB: Foss and Mish. I saw them, Ray, just now,
running for their lives.

RAY: But you're not running.

CABB: Insider info, Ray, insider info.

RAY: I'm sorry?

CABB: Trouble starts at half past ten.
The X-Gang got a challenge from the Slashers
to settle it right here.

RAY: What, on this bench?

CABB: This bench is Slasher territory.

RAY: It is?

CABB: Yeah but it's disputed. See these marks?
    X-Gang members: Tonk, Coster, Spaceman…
    Nigel, but he left.

RAY: Well, it's twenty past.
    Won't they be arriving?

CABB: Ray, my man,
    they're probably here now. Anyway, *I'm* here,
    because Miss Stubborn here –

JAZ: Hi, Ray…

RAY: Howdy.

CABB: Because Miss Stubborn here, she heard about you
    sitting here alone on Valentine's,
    and asked if she could –

RAY: Oh, is it Valentine's?
    (*They thought he knew that.*)

CABB: Is it? Yes – of course, didn't you – can't you –
    can't you feel the love in the air?

JAZ: How are you, Ray?

RAY: A little surprised.

JAZ: Don't be surprised, be cool…

CABB: Jaz is my woman, Ray, I ought to remind you.

JAZ: I'm no one's woman, Ray, don't you mind that loser.
    You heard yourself, you loser? Time to move on,
    it won't be Valentine's soon.

CABB: You watch it, Jaz.

JAZ: Watch what?

CABB: You watch your mouth.

JAZ: Or you'll do what
    exactly?

CABB: You don't know?

JAZ: No, do tell me.

RAY: Could I just ask exactly what you want here?

JAZ: It's you, I don't want him,
    that slob, that saddo, that fool, that tired old –

CABB: Jaz,
    that wasn't in the rehearsal.

JAZ: Why don't you slide
out of the picture here? I do believe
it's past your bedtime, Cabb.

CABB: You bitch, don't do this.

RAY: Plus there's the fight, remember, is it the Slappers
who need this bench?

CABB: The Slashers, Ray, the Slashers,
you woman-stealing bastard.

RAY: Then there's the Egg Gang.

CABB: X, X, for Christ's sake! They'll kill you!

RAY: I don't think so, I've no quarrel with them.

CABB: They'll kill you 'cause you're sitting there, you bastard,
and if they don't I will do!

JAZ: (*To CABB.*) Oi, cool it.

CABB: You're always only playing.
You'd never be my girlfriend in real life,
you probably like *girls*. Don't worry, Ray,
she doesn't really want you.
(*CABB goes off in a huff, back to the gang.*)

RAY: He's angry,
but nothing else was clear.

JAZ: It's clear to me.
He just can't take it, Ray, the way my feelings
changed so quickly.

RAY: Right…
I'm rather worried, though.

JAZ: About us two?

RAY: Us two? Oh no, just you. I'm rather worried
you haven't been 'done in' three times, you know,
by the Egg and Bacon Gang.

JAZ: They never come
before eleven. He's trying to scare you, Ray.
We're all alone.

RAY: I ought to say, I mean I,
I told your boyfriend earlier –

JAZ: My ex.

RAY: Oh, is he in the gang?

JAZ: Ex-boyfriend, Ray.
RAY: Yes, I told him earlier I'm in fact
    waiting for / a girl.
JAZ: / There's no one coming, Ray.
RAY: Maybe he didn't tell you –
JAZ: What I mean is,
    look at the time, my dear.
RAY: Oh yes, she's late,
    but she said she'd come, you know, so all I know
    is that she will. It's the way
    with promises, I'm afraid.
JAZ: And I'm afraid
    whoever makes it breaks it.
RAY: Not this time.
JAZ: Come home with me. I promise
    you'll love it there.
RAY: You do? But you can't do that.
JAZ: I flipping can.
RAY: I'd love it there if I went,
    that's something you can promise, but I can't,
    I can't go, can I?
JAZ: What about my feelings?
RAY: What about – I'm sorry?
JAZ: He says he's sorry.
    Here's my advice to you. Why don't you wait here
    till Valentine's next year for your blasted date?
    And hope the birds will feed you.
    (*JAZ returns to the gang.*)
LUCE: Jaz and Cabb from then began to sulk
    as if they'd really been some sort of item,
    the way they'd been pretending, and Foss laughed
    their plan had gone so wrong. Cabb shut him up
    without a word. And this time
    Mish really started glancing at me, like whose
    fault was it being here? (*To MISH.*) How did I know
    he wouldn't move?

MISH: You could've asked him would he.
    You could've asked him if he'd wait one hour,
    two, three, or four or just sit there forever
    all on his own like making his last stand
    like Colonel Custard up against the Germans.

JAZ: Let's cut our losses, he's a head-case.

LUCE: No,
    it's us who are. He thinks it's worth him waiting,
    but why are we still here?

JAZ: I'll tell you why.
    Because there's only one way we can end this,
    and you're what it is, and I don't know about you lot,
    I want to see you try.

HUTCH: No dice, Chicago.
    I'm…the only way, the way and the light,
    know what I'm saying? Take a back seat, people,
    strap yourselves in and enjoy the ride…
    (*HUTCH strips to the waist and smears mud over his face. Then
    he approaches RAY.*)

LUCE: No one could ever stop him,
    Hutch, whatever he did, and I knew for certain
    I couldn't stop the way it was all now going,
    everything in my life from this one moment,
    like I wasn't allowed to go on with it even until –
    until I was rid of Heidi. But I was Heidi,
    looking across a lawn that sloped away
    towards the pines and instead of seeing a boy
    strolling up with his special invitation,
    I watched that ignoramus, all muddy,
    stumble up with his story.

HUTCH: They got me, Ray,
    the Geezers, look what they did!

RAY: Are you all right?
    They took away your jacket. My friend warned me
    the Slappers might be dangerous but he didn't
    mention any Geezers.

HUTCH: See this mud?

RAY: They threw it at you?

HUTCH: Pushed my face in it.
  Old Geezer trademark but I wouldn't grass.

RAY: They pushed you in the mud and then the grass?

HUTCH: But I wouldn't talk.

RAY: Not even to say 'stop it'?

HUTCH: I'm a broken man.

RAY: Would you like to borrow this jacket?

HUTCH: You saved my life.
  (*RAY passes the orange jacket to HUTCH, who dons it.*)

RAY: It's a sweet colour plus fairly
  warm.

HUTCH: I'm desperate, man, I'm miles from home.
  In fact, I got no home, I never had none.

RAY: That's awful, but it's warm. Heidi did say to
  wear it, but I'm sure she'll understand this.

HUTCH: You saved my life. I'm off now.
  (*HUTCH makes off with the jacket.*)

RAY: Oh, you're going.
  Can you post the jacket back though, that's to Fifteen
  Kimpton Crescent, please!

HUTCH: In your dreams, sucker!
  (*RAY is left in his shirt. He stands up and then sits down.
  HUTCH is back with the gang. LUCE is horrified.*)
  One orange jacket: check. One ice-cold idiot:
  check. Don't mention it. I give him a minute.

LUCE: Give me the jacket, Hutch!

HUTCH: Woah, she wants orange!
  (*CABB intervenes and LUCE is given the jacket. HUTCH,
  sullen, puts his clothes back on.*)

LUCE: (*To us.*) I had to touch it but I was afraid to touch it.
  It had fallen out of a bad dream, my dream,
  but I didn't want it in Hutch's hands.

CABB: One minute.
  And has he shifted? No.

FOSS: He hasn't shifted,
  has he, Cabb? He's stood up and sat down
  but that's it in terms of shifting.

HUTCH: I do hate him,
   I really do, when I said I did it was only
   saying I did but it's now it's saying *and* doing.
JAZ: Why don't you get his shirt, and why stop there,
   his trousers, Hutch?
LUCE: We've got to give it him back,
   he'll catch his death!
JAZ: Whose fault is that?
FOSS: Two minutes.
JAZ: And Luce on a manslaughter charge.
HUTCH: It's his fault.
LUCE: It is in a way, he must know she won't come!
HUTCH: He knows, he knows, he's having a go.
FOSS: It's like
   he's testing us.
CABB: He's not, he's a simpleton.
FOSS: Whatever he is, he's simple.
CABB: He's a throw-back.
   He thinks a promise means you have to do it.
MISH: That is what it means.
CABB: Wrong, it's what it did do,
   Mish, that's all gone out, 'cause otherwise
   you'd never get things done, be always thinking
   'What did I promise, and who to?'
LUCE: I promised
   to meet him here!
FOSS: No, Heidi did.
LUCE: I'm Heidi!
   I'm Heidi. So. I'll tell him.
   I'll tell him about it all. That there's no Heidi.
   I killed her. So. Why don't you all go home?
JAZ: No way, *Jose.*
HUTCH: No dice, LA.
CABB: No, Luce.
   we want to see this finished.
FOSS: Yeah, by you.
MISH: And then we can forget about it.

FOSS: For always,
    always forget about it.

JAZ: He's your baby,
    poor little rich girl.

CABB: Ride in on a pony
    and put him out of his misery.

LUCE: I'm ready.
    (*LUCE prepares to go.*)

HUTCH: No way are you taking the orange jacket.

LUCE: Why not,
    it's his.

HUTCH: Yeah, but I took it, so it looks like
    you wasted me. Don't want that on my record.

LUCE: I'll say I found it, Hutch.

CABB: You threw it away,
    right? because you're tough.

HUTCH: Well I dunno.

CABB: She'll say that if he asks, okay?

HUTCH: I ditched it,
    didn't need it anyroad.

JAZ: Go on, Luce,
    give him his wretched coat and give him the low-down.
    (*LUCE goes to the bench and sits down by RAY.*)

LUCE: (*To us.*) So here I sat, this very same cold bench,
    and there he was, and in the gap between us
    all our letters... Ray,
    are you from school? I mean – it's you from school.

RAY: Hi, are you Lucy, yes?

LUCE: Yes, I'm Lucy, yes,
    from school. I met some other friends from school,
    they said I'd find you here.

RAY: That would be either
    the mixed-up two, the sulking one, the girl
    with the warm home or the one – is that my jacket?

LUCE: It is, it's here, I found it on a branch,
    as if someone had ditched it, didn't need it.
    (*RAY puts the jacket back on.*)

RAY: That's better, warmer. You see it's not my jacket.
  Are most of those your friends?
LUCE: They're mostly hmm,
  they've all been here and there.
RAY: It's very strange.
LUCE: Oh no, we all live here, it's mostly why
  we're mates, you see we're neighbours, we all met
  at sort of garden – functions.
RAY: Garden functions.
LUCE: That's right but you're from where, you're not from here.
RAY: No, I'm a visitor, Lucy.
LUCE: You can call me –
  Luce if it – Luce if it helps. I mean it saves time.
RAY: I've got all the time in the world.
LUCE: There's school tomorrow.
RAY: I won't have to wait that long.
LUCE: They did – they told me,
  one of my friends, about, about you waiting
  for someone –
RAY: Heidi.
LUCE: Heidi.
RAY: Heidi Mirando.
LUCE: Oh her, Heidi Mirando. Is she at school?
RAY: Oh no, not ours. She lives
  some way away and goes to a separate school,
  which can't be all that close, she has to walk there
  over those fields. She talks about her journey,
  which must be nice in spring. I'm saving up
  to go and visit the area.
LUCE: Oh, what area?
RAY: Where she is. She doesn't say.
LUCE: Why don't you
  ask her?
RAY: That's the mystery. I can't
  speak to her. I don't know the address.
  I suppose it's what she wants but I do wonder.
  And I'd like to see her home, it really does sound

elegant and with ornamental gardens,
a tennis pitch they've got and a goldfish pool
plus carved fish. There's a gravel walk to the house
and that's got chandeliers. She lives upstairs
and seems to have to keep herself to herself.
They said they knew her. Do you?
LUCE: Do I – know her?
RAY: Heidi, yes.
LUCE: I do but not to speak to.
RAY: Have you ever tried to?
LUCE: Never but I've been close,
   seen her go by.
RAY: On a horse perhaps, she has one.
LUCE: Yes on a horse, a black one.
RAY: Yes, a black one.
LUCE: Rascal, it's called, I think.
RAY: That's right, so you must have
   been quite near the place.
LUCE: No, she was riding
   not far from here, in fact. I know the name is –
   is Rascal, 'cause I heard her say, 'Good boy,
   well done…Rascal.'
RAY: Oh, and her voice is high
   like that?
LUCE: I can't do voices. Yes it is though.
RAY: And that was here, nearby?
LUCE: It was, on Haddow Lane.
RAY: He's a strong horse
   perhaps. It's a real mystery. And now,
   she's been so very late. I'm very worried.
LUCE: That she won't come?
RAY: Of course she'll come if she can,
   but what if something's happened, maybe she fell,
   was hurt –
LUCE: No, nothing's happened.
   I'm sure she's fine.
RAY: I'm sure as well. She'll come.

LUCE: Ray.

RAY:　　　　Lucy. Luce, sorry, save some time!

LUCE: I heard a rumour lately.

RAY:　　　　　　　　　What's the rumour?

LUCE: The rumour is, there's someone,
　　　there's someone who's not Heidi,
　　　who wants to make you think in a way she is,
　　　is Heidi, who knows why, but so she does that,
　　　pretends her name is Heidi –

RAY:　　　　　　　　　　　That sounds cruel.

LUCE: It is, it's terribly cruel and hurtful.

RAY:　　　　　　　　　　　　Meanwhile
　　　I suppose she's in the dark about this?

LUCE:　　　　　　　　　　Dark?
　　　Who's in the dark?

RAY:　　　　　　Heidi. The real Heidi.

LUCE: Ray, the rumour is –

RAY:　　　　　　　　Behind her back,
　　　that's quite unfair.

LUCE:　　　　　　I agree with that, but Ray.
　　　Ray.

RAY:　　The person couldn't fool me. I know
　　　enough now about Heidi. How unfair.

LUCE: It is, unfair and dreadful, but the rumour,
　　　the rumour is she's stopped, she's realised,
　　　the person, so it's over now.

RAY:　　　　　　　　　Thank goodness.
　　　Now Heidi can forget about it.

LUCE:　　　　　　　　　She never
　　　knew about it, Ray.

RAY:　　　　　　　Then I shan't tell her.

LUCE: When she comes…

RAY:　　　　　　　　When she comes…

LUCE:　　　　　　　　　　　　I'm going,
　　　Ray, I have to, I have to sleep, I need –
　　　it's very late.

RAY: They say there's trouble brewing.
    Nigel carved his name but now he's left.
    The Slappers want him back and the Bacon Boys
    they want to sit right here.

LUCE: Good night, Ray.

RAY: Good night, Luce. Should I mention you to Heidi?

LUCE: No, it's all right. No – if you would, perhaps,
    tell her I'm sorry I didn't speak that time.
    I'd like to be her friend.

RAY: She does need friends.
    All alone in the mansion.

LUCE: Yes she's alone.

RAY: She loses herself in books, though, that's the thing.
    (*LUCE returns to the gang.*)

LUCE: (*To us.*) You all have friends, I can see them. Ask your friends,
    your favourite five and when you're done with them
    ask yourself – would you have told him? Mine,
    mine were unanimous.

CABB: Well that was corking.
    'Carved fish,' he goes, they were dolphins pure and simple.

MISH: And he said there's a tennis pitch, that was my idea,
    but I never said pitch!

CABB: Pathetic.

FOSS: Well-pathetic.
    Anyone knows it ain't a tennis pitch.
    It's a tennis…anyone knows.

CABB: It's all pathetic. Where does he think he comes from?

HUTCH: He wants a kicking.

MISH: He needs a psychopath.

JAZ: A night in the sack.

CABB: And I'm sure you're just the one
    to show him how – why don't you try again?

JAZ: I'd sooner him than you.

MISH: He's a sad case,
    I'm sorry for him, Jaz.

FOSS: So go and snog him.

CABB: You'll have to join the queue, you dozy cow.

JAZ: You leave her alone, you thug.

FOSS: He ain't a thug!

HUTCH: No I seen thugs, this man checks out.

FOSS: Hey Cabb,
    Jaz and Mish are an item!

JAZ: Fly away,
    you little tosser.

FOSS: Don't call me little.

JAZ: You little
    mainstream tosser.

FOSS: You sort her, Cabb!

CABB: Not worth it.
    I'm gonna slide, I'm bored of the lot of you.

FOSS: Me too, the lot of you, except Cabb and Hutch.

HUTCH: I gotta be some place, can't say no more.

CABB: Come on, you guys, let's get irregular.
    Leave 'em in their fairy tale.

FOSS: Yeah… Fairies!
    (*CABB, FOSS and HUTCH go.*)

MISH: You chucking him then, Jaz?

JAZ: Eh?

MISH: Chucking Cabb.

JAZ: He's not my boyfriend, Mish. Nothing to chuck.
    You interested?

MISH: Oh no, just thought I'd check.
    We going home then, Jaz?

JAZ: My mind's in bed
    already.

MISH: What about her?

JAZ: You with us, Heidi?
    Ready to wave goodbye?
    (*JAZ and MISH go.*)

LUCE: (*To us.*)   I didn't know.
    I felt so weak and tired by then I was ready
    to go with anything. Jaz and Mish were leaving,
    I went with that. They hardly spoke to me.
    It was like I'd done some awful deed, they were walking

on ahead so that when I reached my turning
I knew I should say good night, but I didn't say it
and they didn't turn but they knew I lived there, I mean,
we'd all been there together in the kitchen
on that same Valentine's on that same evening,
and I'd made tea in my brand new animal mugs.
It seemed so long ago. And by the time
I realised I'd turned round in a circle
and was going back to the field, I was there already,
hiding in a different garden. I almost
I thought he'd gone, I thought he'd go if I'd gone,
as if I'd imagined him as well! It was just
the mist you get, he was there, Ray, on his bench,
reading his *Just Seventeen*, like after all
the answer might be there.
Now I didn't know, would I stay till he went, is that it?
It felt like it, that I couldn't go till he'd gone now,
that was sort of my fate tonight, but I started
thinking I'd do it now, I'd give him the facts,
I was lifting myself on the wall, I was that prepared,
when I saw what I couldn't believe come out of the mist.
(*JAZ comes back.*)
Her, she'd doubled back, she was trying again!
And I wanted to scream to Ray but she was my friend.
I couldn't let her know I knew she'd done this,
lied to us, betrayed us, come back
thinking we'd all gone. I had to watch her
like I watched everything that awful night,
in silence, listening.
(*JAZ goes to the bench.*)
JAZ: I've got some news for you.
RAY: You often do have,
     your group of friends, you all keep me abreast.
JAZ: It's what we're for. I'm afraid it's not that good.
RAY: Not that good. A rumour, is it?
JAZ: No,
     it's not a rumour, it's real, you know, like news.

It's about a certain Heidi Mirando.

I heard it on the radio.

RAY: The radio?

JAZ: The local radio, yeah. You know she's got
that horse, the black one?

RAY: Rascal, yes.

JAZ: Well, Rascal,
Rascal fell at a fence, right, in her garden,
a fence she was jumping, you know,
she had a bright red jacket on and a cap,
like that and she fell, Heidi, down off her horse
on to her, kind of, head and she's in a coma.
At this moment, a coma at Our Saviour's.

RAY: The hospital?

JAZ: The library, Ray – I'm sorry,
a difficult time for all of us. No Our Saviour's
Hospital for Injuries
to Head, Nose, Throat, Teeth, and…Ears.
Her parents are at her bedside.

RAY: But her father's
in China –

JAZ: He flew back.

RAY: And she has no mother!

JAZ: She – doesn't, does she, no… But someone's there,
some lady, and she cares.

RAY: I don't believe it.
I won't believe it.

JAZ: (*To herself.*) Why not, you bought the rest.

RAY: What shall I do? I'll visit her. These flowers
are plastic, I'll get proper ones –
February, maybe snowdrops? – to remind her
if that would help. Where would they be, I wonder.
No, this is terrible news.

JAZ: I'd leave it, Ray.
She may not recognise you.

RAY: I don't care.
I'll recognise her.

JAZ: Possibly. She sustained
injuries.
RAY: Oh no. Where is Our Saviour's?
JAZ: It's very far away. If I were you
I'd go home and forget about it, I'm sure
someone could use your input.
RAY: Maybe yes.
There's not much I can do.
JAZ: There's truly nothing.
– You gonna leave, then, get up from this bench?
RAY: I'm shocked.
JAZ: Me too I'm gutted. Let's go home.
RAY: She's so, so full of life.
JAZ: You have to stand
and then start walking.
(MISH comes back, surreptitiously, but not surreptitiously enough.)
                What are you doing here?
MISH: Jaz I could ask you that.
JAZ: Then I could tell you.
I'm taking care of Ray.
MISH: That's kind of you,
he's going to need some help. I've just seen Heidi
ice-skating with a boy called Clive!
JAZ: Oh bollocks.
RAY: But that's fantastic!
MISH: Aren't you jealous?
RAY: So it's all
wrong on the radio bulletin!
MISH: On the radio?
Don't think it got on the radio.
RAY: Local radio.
MISH: Amazing.
JAZ: Mish, my star, can I talk to you?
(JAZ and MISH go aside.)
LUCE: That was the last I saw of my friend Jaz.
After that night she was J, just the letter J,
with her older mates and she did still smile at me

but only when no one saw. Mish had a thing
about some Christian boy, so she joined with them,
and went on camps and had a big grin for Jesus,
and always put her arm round me, as if
she'd heard something about me.
  (*The GIRLS come back to RAY.*)
JAZ: Ray, I never heard that on the news.
  I saw it in some film, and for a moment
  everything confused together, you know,
  it does that when it's late, in the modern world,
  then life gets like it could be more exciting.
  There's nothing wrong with Heidi, she's dead healthy.
MISH: Ray, it wasn't Heidi at the rink.
  It must have been Clare Beck who looks the same.
  It was definitely Clive, though, they were dancing
  so wonderfully they could have been on a cake.
  Heidi wasn't there, she was somewhere else.
JAZ: *Ciao, amigo.*
MISH: See ya.
RAY: Good night, you two.
  (*JAZ and MISH go.*)
LUCE: It was sad to see my friends in such a tangle,
  having to take it back, it was brave of them,
  brave in a way, and they didn't know I was there –
  they could have told him everything, just took me
  and torn me up in front of him, a liar,
  Lucy the liar, the cheat, the half of Heidi.
  But they left her still alive. I suppose they felt
  it was still my mess to wash away. I would do.
  I would do and I wish I had but I stayed there,
  cold and crouched and rotten to the middle,
  and waited. As I waited I felt new things,
  crossness with him, Ray, for believing such
  a fairy-tale, a sugary old fable
  I'd made when I was bored,
  for knowing the horse's name and the dad in China,
  the snowdrop field, the dolphins, for believing
  everything I'd chosen!

It's not as if we hadn't all turned up,
the ones who helped with Heidi, we did care!
It's not as if we'd forgotten him, how could we,
we were here hours, you monster! Her name was mine,
but don't forget the rest – they were my friends!
Mish and her tennis pitch, the lawn was Jaz's,
she picked the statues specially from pictures.
The lads had made a map of the house, and Hutch
he'd drawn the father's sports car, it was purple.
But it was all spoiled now. You couldn't have it
being believed like he believed it, 'cause then,
'cause then you'd have this huge great empty gap,
this ash where there's no house and miles of weeds
where there's no gardens either – and where there's
no Heidi, Lucy, me, me being someone
who's not enough, forever, not enough.
(*CABB, FOSS and HUTCH come back. They approach RAY.*
HUTCH adopts a threatening and vaguely oriental posture.)
I didn't even blink when the boys came back.
Where else were they supposed to go?

CABB: Ray.
It's us, it's time.

FOSS: High time.

RAY: High time for what?

CABB: Trouble here.

FOSS: Big trouble here, mainline.

RAY: What's wrong with your friend Hutch?

CABB: Don't catch his eye,
I warn you, Ray, you've pushed the man too far.
You broke the camel's back.

FOSS: That's what you did,
and Hutch don't like that, 'cause he likes…the camel.

RAY: Does he want my jacket back?

CABB: It's too late, Ray.
We've gone beyond.

FOSS: We got no time for jackets.

CABB: We saw the X-Gang gathered in the town…
    they got their masks on and they're in a ring
    and meaning business.
FOSS: Like, 'What do you mean?'
    we asked them, like, and 'business' was the reply…
CABB: Yeah. You have to walk, my friend. I can't
    warn you any further times, you hear me?
RAY: I hear you, you don't understand. My business
    is nothing to do with either them or you two.
FOSS: It is to do with us.
CABB: Shut up. Look, Ray,
    stay any longer, you become their business.
FOSS: You're sitting on their bench.
CABB: And they don't like that.
    They said that, Ray, they know you're here.
RAY: I promised,
    I did already tell you, that I'd wait here.
FOSS: Fine, but you're gonna die.
CABB: He's not gonna die,
    probably, when they get him but he'll get hurt
    possibly, badly.
RAY: I don't believe that's true.
CABB: You don't believe that's true.
    Can I ask you something? What makes you believe
    a load of soppy letters from some princess
    who's got some bleeding palace on a hillside,
    and not believe at getting on for midnight
    on someone's turf you might just get a kicking?
RAY: How do you know what I believe?
CABB: You're here.
    You haven't moved for hours.
RAY: But I promised.
    That I believe because I heard myself.
    I heard the words. And I heard Heidi promise.
CABB: What if it wasn't – what if the girl who promised
    not only wasn't Heidi, but those letters

weren't Heidi either, because there *is no Heidi.*
Because there is no Heidi.

RAY: Somebody promised.
That person promised to come.

FOSS: What if she never?
Never meant it – like said it but not meant it.
It's only a word, you know, six, seven letters…

CABB: What if she doesn't know what it means?

FOSS: Yeah, seven.

CABB: Know what I'm saying?

RAY: You didn't hear her say it.

FOSS: Might've done, like, might've overheard it,
like through a wall.

RAY: It wasn't made to you,
was it?

FOSS: No, all right, but I'd never believe it.

RAY: Perhaps that's why it's never made to you.

CABB: A wall is right, like talking to a wall.
She isn't coming, you're going to get some trouble
because you won't get off this bench, you hear me?
That's the only reason. They don't hate you,
the X-Gang –

FOSS: Some of them hate him.

CABB: But it's not –
it's not the reason, right? It's that you don't
belong on this, you get it?

RAY: Who belongs
anywhere? I didn't ask to be here.

CABB: Then go, go, it's your last chance, Ray, please
go!

RAY: You go, you've got to, I know you do.

CABB: We got to, you're right – Don't be hard on 'em, Ray,
they're okay kids but they gotta do this –

RAY: I know,
they've got to be here, that's what we have in common.

CABB: It's the only thing.

FOSS: Let's go, I can feel 'em, Cabb,
they're coming through the gardens!

(*CABB, FOSS and HUTCH go.*)

LUCE: (*To us.*) But in the gardens there was only me,
    listening, with my cold hands on my cheeks,
    trying to remember the voice in which I said
    'I promise' but it was gone now, there was just this
    mock and a hiss – promise, like Foss said
    just seven letters, that's all, old English word.
    I was going to have to tell him, make it known
    exactly what I'd been and always will be,
    this half a friend of no one. Then they appeared,
    (*CABB, FOSS and HUTCH come back, masked.*)
    three of them, in the mist, and all in plastic
    masks like politician masks I think,
    this gang Cabb knew about, this – the X-Gang.
    Someone tonight had actually told the truth.
    He was in trouble. You see, I'd never been
    out so late so I'd never seen our town
    I mean its night-time face, it's under-side.
    But there they were, moving toward him, I tried
    to shout out 'Ray' – I did, I shouted it out
    'RAY!' but he didn't budge and the gang members
    came on and on, half-hidden in the mist,
    not caring who cried out, and then they reached him.
    (*The BOYS stand around RAY.*)
    You and your friends are thinking it was them,
    I know you are – my friends, and a while later
    I wondered that, only, when it was all, all over,
    I saw the gang run off and as they ran they
    fell down together and fought, punching and kicking,
    till all their masks came off, but in the mist
    I couldn't see a thing that far away though.
    And Cabb and Foss and Hutch well they were friends,
    friends wouldn't have done that.
    (*RAY is beaten up by the BOYS.*)
                So I don't know,
    so I don't think so, although I'd have to tell you
    they also seemed in time to drift apart.

Cabb and Foss were never the friends they were.
Cabb's quite different now, he's got a bike,
you see him down the town with his blue helmet
with some real gang, and Hutch has left, he's gone
to some specific school for ones like him,
and Foss, well just he always hangs around,
staring at me, looking away, he wants
to leave the place, no point in him hanging on.
Is it over yet? Can I look now?
(*The BOYS let RAY fall to the ground, then they run off.*)
I don't know who they were.

RAY: No I don't know.
I was sitting in their place.

LUCE: Well you still are,
and they've all run away.

RAY: My nose is bleeding.

LUCE: Not too badly. – Ray, it's me, the person.
I'm the one who promised, I'm the one,
the girl who wrote the letters, I'm the person.

RAY: This arm is very sore, I can't yet move it.

LUCE: It's me, you see, that's me, all that, that – Heidi–

RAY: It moves a little.

LUCE: I came, you see, I promised.
you knew I'd come and I have.

RAY: Yes, I can go now.
(*Gingerly RAY stands up.*)

LUCE: But can you stand? Don't go –

RAY: Yes, I can stand,
just. Yes, I can stand, I have good knees.

LUCE: But you're too weak to walk –

RAY: No, I can make it.
Here I go.

LUCE: Please stay.

RAY: It's very late.
Lucy, you see, it's really, very.

LUCE: Heidi,
call me, if you want –

RAY: It's going to take me
   longer to get home than normally, but
   that won't take forever.

LUCE: Say something,
   something about Heidi – did you want
   to see the dolphins, Ray, and the field of snowdrops,
   we could, like look for them, we could find them, Ray!
   Don't go, please stay.

RAY: There's school tomorrow morning,
   that's where you have to be. You'd better hurry,
   it's as good as tomorrow now.

LUCE: It is tomorrow.
   (*RAY goes.*)
   Of all the last words in the whole world,
   those were the last three words I said to Ray.
   When his parents saw the state of him, they flipped
   and moved him to a boarding-school. You see him
   sometimes in the holidays. I saw him
   reading in the coach station and wondered
   what he was reading, I hid behind a pillar
   when he went past then only this last weekend
   out sitting by the sailing lake, and with him
   there was this girl with sort of dark red hair,
   done up in ribbons, probably his sister,
   but anyway it really made me angry,
   but not for me, for Heidi, and I know it's
   it's mad but she won't sleep, and I can see her
   sitting there at her window in the moonlight,
   picking out the threads of the straw figure
   her father made her, then looking down at the driveway,
   at the statues on the lawn, the guests arriving,
   and not recognising anyone, but still
   she's trying with all her might.

WWW.OBERONBOOKS.COM

www.ingramcontent.com/pod-product-compliance
Ingram Content Group UK Ltd.
Pitfield, Milton Keynes, MK11 3LW, UK
UKHW020722280225
455688UK00012B/464